FOR A LIBERTARIAN
COMMUNISM

Revolutionary Pocketbooks

FOR A LIBERTARIAN COMMUNISM

Daniel Guérin

Edited and introduced by David Berry

Translation by Mitchell Abidor

For a Libertarian Communism
Daniel Guérin
Editor: David Berry • Translator: Mitchell Abidor
This edition copyright © 2017 PM Press

ISBN: 978-1-62963-236-0
Library of Congress Control Number: 2016948151

Cover by John Yates/Stealworks
Layout by Jonathan Rowland based on work by briandesign

10 9 8 7 6 5 4 3 2 1

PM Press
PO Box 23912
Oakland, CA 94623
www.pmpress.org

Printed in the USA by the Employee Owners of Thomson-Shore in Dexter, Michigan. www.thomsonshore.com

■ CONTENTS

■ FOREWORD AND ACKNOWLEDGMENTS

David Berry

This volume contains a selection of texts by the French revolution-
ary activist and historian Daniel Guérin (1904–1988), published here
in English translation for the first time. They were written between
the 1950s and 1980s and appeared in France in a series of collections:
Jeunesse du socialisme libertaire [Youth of Libertarian Socialism] (Paris:
Rivière, 1959), *Pour un Marxisme libertaire* [For a Libertarian Marxism]
(Paris: Laffont, 1969), and *À la recherche d'un communisme libertaire*
[In Search of a Libertarian Communism] (Paris: Spartacus, 1984).
A further version of the collection was published after his death:
Pour le communisme libertaire [For Libertarian Communism] (Paris:
Spartacus, 2003). All of these contain slightly different selections
of texts around a common core of recurrent pieces, and the same
is true of this English edition. We have tried to choose those texts
which would be of most interest to present-day readers, but which
also give a good understanding of Guérin's developing analysis of
the failings of the Left and of his belief that the only way forward
was through some kind of synthesis of Marxism and anarchism.

We are grateful to the Spartacus collective, to Daniel Guerrier,
and to Anne Guérin for permission to publish these translations.

The footnotes are Guérin's except where indicated; additional
explanatory material is followed by my initials. We have tried
(where possible and practical) to provide references to English
translations of Guérin's sources, and I am grateful to Iain McKay
for his help with this. I would also like to thank Chris Reynolds,
Martin O'Shaughnessy, and Christophe Wall-Romana for their help
in tracking down the source of Guérin's reference to Armand Gatti;

and Danny Evans and James Yeoman for their advice regarding films about the Spanish Revolution.

Guérin was a prolific writer on an exceptionally wide range of topics, and relatively little has been translated into English. A list of his publications in English can be found at the end of the volume. For further information, including a full bibliography and links to texts available online, please visit the website of the Association des Amis de Daniel Guérin (the Association of the Friends of Daniel Guérin) at www.danielguerin.info.

■ LIST OF ACRONYMS

AL	Alternative Libertaire (Libertarian Alternative), founded 1991
CFDT	Confédération Française Démocratique du Travail (Democratic French Labour Confederation), founded 1964
CGT	Confédération Générale du Travail (General Labour Confederation), founded 1895
CGTU	Confédération Générale du Travail Unitaire (Unitary General Labour Confederation), 1921–1936
CNT	Confédération Nationale du Travail (National Labour Confederation), founded 1946
FA	Fédération Anarchiste (Anarchist Federation), founded 1945
FCL	Fédération Communiste Libertaire (Libertarian Communist Federation), 1953–1957
FEN	Fédération de l'Education Nationale (National Education Federation), 1948–1992
FO	Force Ouvrière (Workers' Power), founded 1947
FSU	Fédération Syndicale Unitaire (Unitary Trade Union Federation), founded 1992
JAC	Jeunesse Anarchiste Communiste (Communist Anarchist Youth), founded 1967

OCL	Organisation Communiste Libertaire (Libertarian Communist Organization), founded 1976
ORA	Organisation Révolutionnaire Anarchiste (Anarchist Revolutionary Organization), 1967–1976
PCF	Parti Communiste Français (French Communist Party), founded 1920
PCI	Parti Communiste Internationaliste (Internationalist Communist Party), 1944–1968
PS-SFIO	Parti Socialiste—Section Française de l'Internationale Ouvrière (Socialist Party, French Section of the Workers' International), 1905–1969
PSOP	Parti Socialiste Ouvrier et Paysan (Workers' and Peasants' Socialist Party), 1938–1940
SUD	Solidaires, Unitaires, Démocratiques (Solidarity, Unity, Democracy), founded 1988
UGAC	Union des Groupes Anarchistes-Communistes (Union of Communist-Anarchist Groups), 1961–1968
UTCL	Union des travailleurs communistes libertaires (Union of Libertarian Communist Workers), 1974–1991

■ THE SEARCH FOR A LIBERTARIAN COMMUNISM:

DANIEL GUÉRIN AND THE "SYNTHESIS" OF MARXISM AND ANARCHISM

> I have a horror of sects, of compartmentalisation, of people who are separated by virtually nothing and who nevertheless face each other as if across an abyss.
> —Daniel Guérin[1]

As he once wrote of the fate suffered by anarchism, Daniel Guérin (1904–1988) has himself been the victim of unwarranted neglect and, in some circles at least, of undeserved discredit. For although many people know of Guérin, relatively few seem aware of the breadth of his contribution. His writings cover a vast range of subjects, from fascism and the French Revolution to the history of the European and American labour movements; from Marxist and anarchist theory to homosexual liberation; from French colonialism to the Black Panthers; from Paul Gauguin to French nuclear tests in the Pacific—not to mention several autobiographical volumes. As an activist, Guérin was involved in various movements and campaigns: anticolonialism, antiracism, antimilitarism, and homosexual liberation. This is a man who counted among his personal friends François Mauriac, Simone Weil, C.L.R. James, and Richard Wright, to name but a few of the famous names which litter his autobiographies. His youthful literary efforts provoked a letter of congratulation from Colette; he met and corresponded with Leon Trotsky; and he had dinner "en tête à tête" with Ho Chi Minh. Jean-Paul Sartre

A version of this introduction was first published in Alex Prichard, Ruth Kinna, Saku Pinta, and David Berry (eds.), *Libertarian Socialism: Politics in Black and Red* (Basingstoke: Palgrave Macmillan, 2012; 2nd edition, Oakland: PM Press, 2017).

judged his reinterpretation of the French Revolution to be "one of the only contributions by contemporary Marxists to have enriched historical studies."[2] The gay liberation activist Pierre Hahn believed his own generation of homosexuals owed more to Guérin than to any other person, and the Martinican poet Aimé Césaire paid tribute to his work on decolonization. Noam Chomsky considers Guérin's writings on anarchism to be of great importance to the development of contemporary socialist thought.

Yet despite such assessments, and although there is widespread and enduring interest in Guérin among activists, he has been badly neglected by academic researchers in France and especially in the English-speaking world. This is doubtless due to a combination of factors: Guérin never held an academic post or any leadership position (except briefly at the Liberation as director of the Commission du Livre, a government agency that oversaw the book publishing industry); he was consistently anti-Stalinist during a period when the influence of the French Communist Party, both among intellectuals and within the labour movement, was overwhelming; he never fit easily into ideological or political pigeonholes and was often misunderstood and misrepresented; and in France in the 1960s and 1970s, his bisexuality was shocking even for many on the Left. Guérin was, in a word, a "troublemaker."[3]

Concerned that his reinterpretation of the French Revolution, *La Lutte de classes sous la Première République, 1793–1797* (1946), had been misunderstood, in 1947, Daniel Guérin wrote to his friend, the socialist Marceau Pivert, that the book was to be seen as "an introduction to a synthesis of anarchism and Marxism-Leninism I would like to write one day."[4] What exactly did Guérin mean by this "synthesis," and how and why had he come to be convinced of its necessity? For as Alex Callinicos has commented, "genuinely innovative syntheses are rare and difficult to arrive at. Too often attempted syntheses amount merely to banality, incoherence, or eclecticism."[5]

It must however be noted from the outset that Guérin had no pretensions to being a theorist: he saw himself first and foremost as an activist and secondly as a historian.[6] Indeed, from the day in 1930 when he abandoned the poetry and novels of his youth, all his research and writings were concerned more or less directly with his political commitments.[7] His developing critique of Marxism and his later interest in the relationship between Marxism and anarchism were motivated by his own direct experience of active participation in revolutionary struggles on a number of fronts; they can thus only be clarified when studied in relation to social and political developments.

Although Guérin, in some of his autobiographical or semi-autobiographical writings, had a tendency to divide his life into more or less distinct "phases," and despite the fact that his political or ideological trajectory may seem to some to be rather protean, I would argue that there was in fact an underlying ideological consistency—even if changing circumstances meant that his "organisational options" (as he put it) changed in different periods of his life. A historical materialist all his life, he remained attached to a revolutionary socialism with a strong ethical or moral core. Although it was many years before he found an organisation which lived up to his expectations, he was always at heart a libertarian communist, developing an increasingly strong belief in the need for a "total revolution" which would attach as much importance to issues of race, gender, and sexuality as to workplace-based conflict. Whether specifically in his commitment to anticolonialism or to sexual liberation, or more generally in his emphasis on what today would be called intersectionality, Guérin was undoubtedly ahead of his time.

Early Influences

Despite coming from the "*grande bourgeoisie*"—a background which he would come to reject—Guérin owed much to the influence of his branch of the family: humanist, liberal and cultured, both his parents had been passionately pro-Dreyfus, both were influenced by Tolstoy's ethical and social ideas, and his father's library contained *The Communist Manifesto* as well as works by Benoît Malon, Proudhon, and Kropotkin.[8] The young Daniel seems to have been particularly influenced by his father's pacifism and was also deeply affected by his own reading of Tolstoy's *Diaries* and *Resurrection*.[9] In the context of the increasingly polarised debates of the inter-war period between the Far Right and Far Left ("Maurras *versus* Marx" as he put it), he identified with the "Marxist extreme Left" from a relatively early age.[10] His later "discovery" of the Parisian working class and of the concrete realities of their everyday existence (to a large extent through his homosexual relationships with young workers) reinforced a profound "workerism" which would stay with him for the rest of his life.[11]

The Bankruptcy of Stalinism and Social Democracy

This workerism would lead him in 1930–1931 to join the syndicalists grouped around the veteran revolutionary Pierre Monatte: typically, perhaps, Guérin's first real active involvement was in the campaign for the reunification of the two major syndicalist confederations, the CGT (dominated at that time by the PS-SFIO, the Socialist Party) and the CGTU (dominated by the PCF, the French Communist Party). His workerism was also responsible for a strong attraction towards the PCF, far more "proletarian" than the Socialist Party, despite his "visceral anti-Stalinism" and what he saw as the Party's "crass ideological excesses, its inability to win over the majority of workers, and its mechanical submission to the Kremlin's orders."[12] Yet Guérin was no more impressed with the PS, which he found petty-bourgeois, narrow-minded, dogmatically anticommunist, and obsessed with electioneering:

> The tragedy for many militants of our generation was our repugnance at having to opt for one or the other of the two main organisations which claimed, wrongly, to represent the working class. Stalinism and social democracy both repelled us, each in its own way. Yet those workers who were active politically were in one of these two parties. The smaller, intermediate groups and the extremist sects seemed to us to be doomed to impotence and marginalisation. The SFIO, despite the social conformism of its leadership, at least had the advantage over the Communist Party of enjoying a certain degree of internal democracy, and to some extent allowed revolutionaries to express themselves; whereas the monolithic automatism of Stalinism forbade any critics from opening their mouths and made it very difficult for them even to stay in the party.[13]

Hence his decision to rejoin the SFIO in 1935, shortly before the creation by Marceau Pivert of the *Gauche* révolutionnaire (Revolutionary

Left) tendency within the party, of which he would become a leading member. Guérin was attracted by Pivert's "Luxemburgist," libertarian and syndicalist tendencies.[14] He was consistently on the revolutionary wing of the *Gauche révolutionnaire* and of its successor, the *Parti socialiste ouvrier et paysan* (PSOP, or Workers' and Peasants' Socialist Party, created when the GR was expelled from the SFIO in 1938), and, in the Popular Front period, he drew a clear distinction between what he called the "Popular Front no. 1"—an electoral alliance between social democracy, Stalinism, and bourgeois liberalism—and the "Popular Front no. 2"—the powerful, extra-parliamentary, working-class movement, which came into conflict with the more moderate (and more bourgeois) Popular Front government.[15] He viewed the "entryism" of the French Trotskyists in these years as a welcome counterbalance to the reformism of the majority of the Socialist Party.[16]

Indeed, in the 1930s, Guérin agreed with Trotsky's position on many issues: on the nature of fascism and how to stop it; on war and revolutionary proletarian internationalism; on opposition to the collusion between "social-patriotism" (i.e., mainstream social democracy) and "national-communism" (i.e., the PCF) as well as any pact with the bourgeois Radicals; and on the need to fight actively for the liberation of Europe's colonies. As Guérin comments after recounting in glowing terms his sole meeting with Trotsky in Barbizon (near Fontainebleau) in 1933: "On a theoretical level as well as on the level of political practice, Trotsky would remain, for many of us, both a stimulus to action and a teacher."[17]

Ultimately, Guérin's experience of the labour movement and of the Left in the 1930s—as well as his research on the nature and origins of fascism and Nazism[18]—led him to reject both social democracy and Stalinism as effective strategies for defeating fascism and preventing war. Indeed, the Left—"divided, ossified, negative, and narrow-minded" in Guérin's words—bore its share of responsibility and had made tragic errors.[19] The SFIO was criticised by Guérin for its electoralism and for allowing its hands to be tied by the *Parti radical-socialiste*, "a bourgeois party whose corruption and bankruptcy were in large part responsible for the fascist explosion"; for its incomprehension of the nature of the capitalist state, which led to the impotence of Léon Blum's 1936 Popular

Front government; for its failure to take fascism seriously (and to aid the Spanish Republicans), despite the warnings, until it was too late; and for its obsessive rivalry with the PCF. The PCF was equally harshly criticised by Guérin—for what seemed to him to be its blind obedience to the Comintern, the criminal stupidity of the Comintern's "third period" and for its counter-revolutionary strategy both in Spain and in France.[20]

As for Trotsky, Guérin disagreed with him over the creation of the Fourth International in 1938, which seemed to him premature and divisive. More generally, Guérin was critical of what he saw as Trotsky's tendency continually to transpose the experiences of the Russian Bolsheviks onto contemporary events in the West, and of his "authoritarian rigidness." Trotskyism, Guérin argued, represented "the ideology of the infallible leader who, in an authoritarian fashion, directs the policy of a fraction or of a party."[21] What Guérin wanted to see was "the full development of the spontaneity of the working class."[22] Writing in 1963, Guérin would conclude with regard to such disputes over revolutionary tactics:

> The revolutionary organisation which was lacking in June 1936 was not, in my opinion, an authoritarian leadership emanating from a small group or sect, but an organ for the coordination of the workers' councils, growing directly out of the occupied workplaces. The mistake of the *Gauche Révolutionnaire* was not so much that it was unable, because of its lack of preparation, to transform itself into a revolutionary party on the Leninist or Trotskyist model, but that it was unable ... to help the working class to find for itself its own form of power structure to confront the fraud that was the Popular Front no. 1.[23]

So as Guérin summarised the state of the Left in the 1930s: "Everything made the renewal of the concepts and methods of struggle employed by the French Left both indispensable and urgent."[24] These debates on the Left regarding tactics (working-class autonomy or "Popular Frontism") and the role of the "avant-garde" or, in syndicalist terms, the "activist minority" (*minorité agissante*) would recur in the postwar years, and Guérin's position would vary little.

The Break from Trotskyism

Despite Guérin's reservations about Trotskyism, his analysis of the nature of the Vichy regime was very similar to that put forward by the Fourth International, and he was also impressed with Trotsky's manifesto of May 1940, "La guerre impérialiste et la révolution prolétarienne mondiale" [Imperialist War and the World Proletarian Revolution], including it in a collection of Trotsky's writings on the Second World War he would edit in 1970.[25] He worked with the Trotskyists in the resistance, not least because they remained true to their internationalism and to their class politics.[26] They rejected, for instance, what Guérin saw as the PCF's demagogic nationalism. Guérin was thus closely involved with the Trotskyists' attempts to organise extremely dangerous anti-militarist and anti-Nazi propaganda among German soldiers. He also contributed to the activities of a group of Trotskyist workers producing newsletters carrying reports of workplace struggles against both French employers and the German authorities.

However, an extended study tour of the United States from 1946 to 1949, which included visits to branches or prominent militants of the Socialist Workers' Party and the breakaway Workers' Party, represented a turning point in Guérin's "Trotskyism." In a 1948 letter to Marceau Pivert, he commented on his unhappiness with the Trotskyists' tendency to "repeat mechanically old formulae without rethinking them, relying lazily and uncritically on the (undeniably admirable) writings of Trotsky."[27] Looking back thirty years later, he would conclude: "It was thanks to the American Trotskyists, despite their undeniable commitment, that I ceased forever believing in the virtues of revolutionary parties built on authoritarian, Leninist lines."[28]

The "Mother of Us All"

Unlike many on the Left associated with postwar ideological renewal, most of whom would focus on a revision or reinterpretation of Marxism, often at a philosophical level (Sartre, Althusser, or Henri Lefebvre, for example), Guérin the historian began with a return to what he saw as the source of revolutionary theory and praxis: in 1946, he published his study of class struggle in the First French Republic (1793–1797).[29] The aim of the book was to "draw lessons from the greatest, longest and deepest revolutionary experience France has ever known, lessons which would help regenerate the revolutionary, libertarian socialism of today," and to "extract some ideas which would be applicable to our time and of direct use to the contemporary reader who has yet to fully digest the lessons of another revolution: the Russian Revolution."[30] Applying the concepts of permanent revolution and combined and uneven development, inspired by Trotsky's *History of the Russian Revolution*, Guérin argued that the beginnings of a conflict of class interest could already be detected within the revolutionary camp between an "embryonic" proletariat—the *bras nus* (manual workers), represented by the *Enragés*—and the bourgeoisie—represented by Robespierre and the Jacobin leadership. For Guérin, the French Revolution thus represented not only the birth of bourgeois parliamentary democracy, but also the emergence of "a new type of democracy," a form of working-class direct democracy as seen, however imperfectly, in the "*sections*" (local popular assemblies), precursors of the Commune of 1871 and the Soviets of 1905 and 1917.[31] In the second edition of the work (1968) he would add "the Commune of May 1968" to that genealogy.

Similarly, this interpretation tended to emphasise the political ambivalence of the bourgeois Jacobin leadership which "hesitated continually between the solidarity uniting it with the popular classes against the aristocracy and that uniting all the wealthy, property-owning classes against those who owned little or nothing."[32] For Guérin, the essential lesson to be drawn from the French Revolution was thus the conflict of class interest between the bourgeoisie and the working classes. Bourgeois, social democratic, and Stalinist interpretations of the Revolution—like those of Jean Jaurès, Albert Mathiez, and so many others—which tended to maintain the "cult of Robespierre" and to reinforce the labour movement's dependence on bourgeois democracy, were thus to be rejected.[33]

Class Struggle in the First Republic has been described by Eric Hobsbawm, himself a longstanding Communist Party member, as "a curious combination of libertarian and Trotskyist ideas—not without a dash of Rosa Luxemburg."[34] It not only shocked many academic historians of the Revolution—especially those with more or less close links to the PCF (Georges Lefebvre, and especially Albert Soboul and George Rudé)—but also those politicians who, in Guérin's words, "have been responsible for perverting and undermining true proletarian socialism."[35] The fallout was intense and the ensuing debate lasted for many years; indeed, Guérin is still today regarded with distrust by many historians influenced by the Republican and mainstream Marxist (non-Trotskyist) interpretations of the Revolution as a bourgeois revolution.[36] Guérin brought that whole historiographical tradition into question. The political significance was that the Revolutionary Terror had been used as a parallel to justify Bolshevik repression of democratic freedoms and repression of more leftist movements. Stalin had been compared to Robespierre. The Jacobin tradition of patriotism and national unity in defence of the bourgeois democratic Republic has been one of the characteristics of the dominant tendencies within the French Left, and therefore central to the political mythologies of the Popular Front and the Resistance. Guérin, as Ian Birchall has put it, "was polemicizing against the notion of a Resistance uniting all classes against the foreign invader."[37]

What is more, the PCF had been campaigning since 1945 for unity at the top with the SFIO, and in the 1956 elections called for the re-establishment of a Popular Front government. Guérin, as we have seen, argued that alliance with the supposedly "progressive" bourgeoisie in the struggle against fascism was a contradiction at the heart of the Popular Front strategy. His conception of the way forward for the Left was very different. At a time when fascism in the form of Poujadism looked as if it might once more be a real threat, Guérin argued that what was needed was a "genuine" Popular Front, that is, a grassroots social movement rather than a governmental alliance, a truly popular movement centred on the working classes that would bring together the labour movement and all socialists who rejected both the pro-American SFIO and the pro-Soviet PCF:

> And if we succeed in building this new Popular Front, let us not
> repeat the mistakes of the 1936 Popular Front, which because of
> its timidity and impotence ended up driving the middle classes
> towards fascism, rather than turning them away from it as had

been its aim. Only a combative Popular Front, which dares to attack big business, will be able to halt our middle classes on the slope which leads to fascism and to their destruction.[38]

The Developing Critique of Leninism

Guérin's friend and translator, C.L.R. James, wrote in 1958 of the political significance of Guérin's revisiting the history of the French Revolution:

> Such a book had never yet been produced and could not have been produced in any epoch other than our own. It is impregnated with the experience and study of the greatest event of our time: the development and then degeneration of the Russian Revolution, and is animated implicitly by one central concern: how can the revolutionary masses avoid the dreadful pitfalls of bureaucratisation and the resurgence of a new oppressive state power, and instead establish a system of direct democracy?[39]

It was in very similar terms that Guérin expressed the central question facing the Left in a 1959 essay, "La Révolution déjacobinisée."[40] This is an important text in Guérin's ideological itinerary, continuing the political analysis he began in *La Lutte de classes sous la Pemière République* and developed in *La Révolution française et nous* [The French Revolution and Us] (written in 1944 but not published until 1969) and "Quand le fascisme nous devançait" [When Fascism Was Winning] (1955).[41]

In "La Révolution déjacobinisée," Guérin argued that the "Jacobin" traits in Marxism and particularly in Leninism were the result of an incomplete understanding on Marx and Engels' part of the class nature of Jacobinism and the Jacobin dictatorship, to be distinguished according to Guérin from the democratically controlled *contrainte révolutionnaire* ("revolutionary coercion") exercised by the popular *sections*. Thus by applying a historical materialist analysis to the experiences of the French revolutionary movement, Guérin came to argue, essentially, that "authentic" socialism (contrary to what had been argued by Blanqui or Lenin) arose spontaneously out of working-class struggle and that it was fundamentally libertarian. Authoritarian conceptions of party organisation and revolutionary strategy had their origins in bourgeois or even aristocratic modes of thought.

Guérin believed that when Marx and Engels referred—rather vaguely—to a "dictatorship of the proletariat" they envisaged it as a dictatorship exercised by the working class as a whole, rather than by an avant-garde. But, he continued, Marx and Engels did not adequately differentiate their interpretation from that of the Blanquists. This made possible Lenin's later authoritarian conceptions: "Lenin, who saw himself as both a 'Jacobin' and a 'Marxist,' invented the idea of the dictatorship of a party substituting itself for the working class and acting by proxy in its name."[42] This, for Guérin, was where it all started to go badly wrong: "The double experience of the French and Russian Revolutions has taught us that this is where we touch upon the central mechanism whereby direct democracy, the self-government of the people, is transformed, gradually, by the introduction of the revolutionary 'dictatorship,' into the reconstitution of an apparatus for the oppression of the people."[43]

Guérin's leftist, class-based critique of Jacobinism thus had three related implications for contemporary debates about political tactics and strategy. First, it implied a rejection of "class collaboration" and therefore of any type of alliance with the bourgeois Left (Popular Frontism). Second, it implied that the revolutionary movement should be uncompromising, that it should push for more radical social change and not stop halfway (which, as Saint-Just famously remarked, was to dig one's own grave), rejecting the Stalinist emphasis on the unavoidability of separate historical "stages" in the long-term revolutionary process. Third, it implied a rejection both of the Leninist model of a centralised, hierarchical party dominating the labour movement and of the "substitutism" (substitution of the party for the proletariat) which had come to characterise the Bolshevik dictatorship.

This critique clearly had its sources both in Guérin's reinterpretation of the French Revolution and in the social and political conditions of the time. *La Révolution française et nous* was informed by Guérin's critique of social democratic and Stalinist strategies before, during, and after the war. "La révolution déjacobinisée" was written at a significant historic moment for socialists in France:

after the artificial national unity of the immediate postwar years had given way to profound social and political conflict; as Guy Mollet's SFIO became increasingly identified with the defence of the bourgeois status quo and the Western camp in the cold war; as the immensely powerful postwar PCF reeled under the effects of the Hungarian uprising of 1956 and of the Khrushchev revelations the same year; and as the unpopular and politically unstable Fourth Republic collapsed in the face of a threatened military coup. It was this situation which made renewal of the Left so necessary. In 1959, Guérin also picked up on the results of a survey of the attitudes of French youth towards politics, which indicated to him two things: first, that what alienated the younger generation from "socialism" was "bureaucrats and purges," and second, that, as one respondent put it, "French youth are becoming more and more anarchist."[44] Ever the optimist, Guérin declared:

> Far from allowing ourselves to sink into doubt, inaction, and despair, the time has come for the French Left to begin again from zero, to rethink its problems from their very foundations. . . . The necessary synthesis of the ideas of equality and liberty . . . cannot and must not be attempted, in my opinion, in the framework and to the benefit of a bankrupt bourgeois democracy. It can and must only be done in the framework of socialist thought, which remains, despite everything, the only reliable value of our times. The failure of both reformism and Stalinism imposes on us the urgent duty to find a way of reconciling (proletarian) democracy with socialism, freedom with Revolution.[45]

From Trotskyism to New Left to Anarchism

What Guérin would thus do which was quite remarkable in post-Liberation France was endeavour to separate Marxism from Bolshevism—his continued friendly and supportive contacts with a number of Trotskyists notwithstanding—and it is noteworthy that he had contact in this period with a number of prominent non-orthodox Marxists. After 1945, especially, he was involved (centrally or more peripherally) in a number of circles or networks, and according to the sociologist Michel Crozier (who, since their meeting in America, saw Guérin as something of a mentor) Guérin self-identified in the late 1940s and early 1950s—"the golden age of the Left intelligentsia"—as an "independent Marxist."[46]

C.L.R. James, for instance, has already been mentioned. He and Guérin appear to have met in the 1930s; they became good friends, Guérin visited him while in the USA in 1949, and they corresponded over many years. Convinced of the contemporary relevance and of the importance of Guérin's analysis, James even began to translate *La Lutte de classes* into English, and described the book as "one of the most important modern textbooks in . . .the study of Marxism" and "one of the great theoretical landmarks of our movement."[47]

Similarly, Guérin had first met Karl Korsch in Berlin in 1932, and visited him in his exile in Cambridge, Massachusetts, in 1947, where according to Guérin they spent many hours together.[48] The two would collaborate a decade later in their bibliographical researches on the relationship between Marx and Bakunin.[49] Also during his time in the USA in 1947, Guérin became friendly with a group of refugee Germans in Washington, D.C., dissident Marxists, "as hospitable as they were brilliant," connected with the so-called Frankfurt School: Franz Neumann, Otto Kirchheimer and Herbert Marcuse.[50]

In France, Guérin already knew the leading figures in the Socialisme ou Barbarie group from their days in the Fourth International's PCI (Internationalist Communist Party) together: Guérin's papers contain a number of texts produced by the so-called Chaulieu-Montal Tendency in the late 1940s.[51] It is interesting to note that the Socialisme ou Barbarie group's theses on the Russian Revolution feature in the list of theories and authors discovered by the Algerian nationalist and revolutionary, Mohammed Harbi, thanks to his first meeting with Guérin (at a meeting of the PCI discussion group, the "Cercle Lénine") in 1953.[52] In 1965 Guérin took part, with Castoriadis, Lefort, and Edgar Morin, in a forum on "Marxism Today" organised by Socialisme ou Barbarie (whose work Morin would describe a few years later as representing "an original synthesis of Marxism and anarchism"[53]). Guérin also contributed to Morin's *Arguments* (1956–1962), an important journal launched in response to the events of 1956 with a view to a "reconsideration not only of Stalinist Marxism, but of the Marxist way of thinking,"[54] and he had been centrally involved with the French "Titoists" around Clara Malraux and the review *Contemporains* (1950–1951).[55]

The present state of our knowledge of these relationships does not enable us to be precise regarding the nature, extent or direction of any influence which might have resulted, but the least we can say is that Guérin was at the heart of the Left-intellectual ferment which characterised these years, that he had an address book, as his daughter Anne recently put it,[56] as fat as a dictionary and that he shared many of the theoretical preoccupations of many leading Marxists in the twenty years or so following the Second World War, be it the party-form, bureaucracy, alienation or sexual repression.

In the mid-to-late 1950s, like other former or "critical" Trotskyists, as well as ex-members of the FCL (the Libertarian Communist Federation, banned in 1956[57]), Guérin belonged—though "without much conviction"—to a series of Left-socialist organisations: the *Nouvelle Gauche* [New Left], the *Union de la Gauche Socialiste* [Union of the Socialist Left], and, briefly, the *Parti Socialiste Unifié* [Unified Socialist Party].[58] But it was also around 1956 that Guérin "discovered" anarchism. Looking back on a 1930 boat trip to Vietnam and the small library he had taken with him, Guérin commented that of all the authors he had studied—Marx, Proudhon, Georges Sorel, Hubert Lagardelle, Fernand Pelloutier, Lenin, Trotsky, Gandhi, and many others—"Marx had, without a doubt, been preponderant."[59] But having become increasingly critical of Leninism, Guérin discovered the collected works of Bakunin, a "revelation" which rendered him forever "allergic to all versions of authoritarian socialism, whether Jacobin, Marxist, Leninist, or Trotskyist."[60] Guérin would describe the following ten years or so (i.e., the mid-1950s to the mid-1960s)—which saw the publication notably of the popular anthology *Ni Dieu ni Maître* and of *L'Anarchisme*, which sold like hotcakes at the Sorbonne in May 1968—as his "classical anarchist phase."[61] He became especially interested in Proudhon, whom he admired as the first theorist of *autogestion*, or worker self-management;[62] Bakunin, representative of revolutionary, working-class anarchism, close to Marxism, Guérin insisted, yet remarkably prescient about the dangers of statist communism; and Max Stirner, appreciated as a precursor of 1968 because of his determination to attack bourgeois prejudice and puritanism.

The discovery of Bakunin coincided with the appearance of the Hungarian workers' committees and the Soviet suppression of the Hungarian uprising in 1956. These events provoked Guérin into studying the councilist tradition, which had come to be seen by many as representing a form of revolutionary socialist direct democracy in contrast to the Bolshevik-controlled *soviets*.[63] It was also during the 1950s that Guérin, moving on from his study of the French Revolution, had begun to research the political debates and conflicts within the First International and more generally the relationship between Marxism and anarchism.

Guérin and Anarchism

Guérin had had no contact with the anarchist movement before the Second World War, other than to read E. Armand's individualist anarchist organ *L'en dehors*.[64] According to Georges Fontenis, a leading figure in the postwar anarchist movement, Guérin began to have direct contact with the then Anarchist Federation (FA) in 1945, when the second edition of his *Fascism and Big Business* was published. The FA's newspaper, *Le Libertaire*, reviewed Guérin's books favourably, and in the 1950s, he was invited to galas of the FA and (from 1953) of the FCL to do book signings. He got to know leading anarchist militants and would drop in at the FCL's offices on the Quai de Valmy in Paris. Fontenis described him as being "an active sympathiser" at that point.[65] His new-found sympathies certainly seem to have been sufficiently well-known for the US embassy in Paris to refuse him a visa to visit his wife and daughter in 1950 on the grounds that he was both a Trotskyist *and* an anarchist.[66] The ideological stance of the FCL ("libertarian Marxism") and its position on the Algerian war ("critical support" for the nationalist movement in the context of the struggle against French bourgeois imperialism) proved doubly attractive to the anticolonialist Guérin.[67] In part for these reasons, 1954 (the beginning of the Algerian war of independence) represented the beginning of a relationship, notably with Fontenis (leading light of the FCL), which as we shall see would ultimately take Guérin into the ranks of the "libertarian communist" movement.

In 1959, Guérin published a collection of articles entitled *Jeunesse du socialisme libertaire*: literally the youth—or perhaps the rise, or invention—of libertarian socialism. This represented both a continuation of the critique of Marxism and Leninism begun during the war, and—as far as I am aware—Guérin's first analysis of the nineteenth-century anarchist tradition. Significantly, a copy of this collection has been found with a handwritten dedication to Maximilien Rubel, "to whom this little book owes so much."[68] A few years later, in 1965, he would publish both *Anarchism: From Theory to Practice* and the two-volume anthology *No Gods No Masters*. The purpose was to "rehabilitate" anarchism, and the anthology represented the "dossier of evidence":

> Anarchism has for many years suffered from an undeserved disrepute, from an injustice which has manifested itself in three ways.
>
> Firstly, its detractors claim that it is simply a thing of the past. It did not survive the great revolutionary tests of our time: the Russian Revolution and the Spanish Revolution. It has no place in the modern world, a world characterised by centralisation, by large political and economic entities, by the idea of totalitarianism. There is nothing left for the anarchists to do but, "by force of circumstance" as Victor Serge put it, to "join the revolutionary Marxists."
>
> Secondly, the better to devalue it, those who would slander anarchism serve up a tendentious interpretation of its doctrine. Anarchism is essentially individualistic, particularistic, hostile to any form of organisation. It leads to fragmentation, to the egocentric withdrawal of small local units of administration and production. It is incapable of centralizing or of planning. It is nostalgic for the "golden age." It tends to resurrect archaic social forms. It suffers from a childish optimism; its "idealism" takes no account of the solid realities of the material infrastructure. It is incurably petit-bourgeois; it places itself outside of the class movement of the modern proletariat. In a word, it is "reactionary."
>
> And finally, certain of its commentators take care to rescue from oblivion and to draw attention to only its most controversial deviations, such as terrorism, individual assassinations, propaganda by explosives and so on.[69]

Although, as we have seen, he referred to the two books (*Anarchism* and *No Gods No Masters*) as representing his "classical anarchist" phase, and despite his assertion that the basics of anarchist doctrine were relatively homogeneous, elsewhere he was very clear that both books focussed on a particular *kind* of anarchism. To begin with, "the fundamental aspect of these doctrines" was, for Guérin, that "*anarchy*, is indeed, above all, synonymous with *socialism*. The anarchist is, first and foremost, a socialist whose aim is to put an end to the exploitation of man by man. Anarchism is no more than one of the branches of socialist thought. . . . For Adolph Fischer, one of the Chicago martyrs, 'every anarchist is a socialist, but every socialist is not necessarily an anarchist.'"[70]

In *Pour un Marxisme libertaire* (1969), Guérin described himself as coming from the school of "anti-Stalinist Marxism," but as having for some time been in the habit of "delving into the treasury of libertarian thought." Anarchism, he insisted, was still relevant and still very much alive, "provided that it is first divested of a great deal of childishness, utopianism and romanticism."[71] He went on to comment that because of this openness towards the contribution of anarchism, his book, *Anarchism*, had been misunderstood by some, and that it did not mean that he had become an "ecumenical" anarchist, to use Georges Fontenis' term.[72] In "Anarchisme et Marxisme" (written in 1973), Guérin emphasised that his book on anarchism had focussed on "social, constructive, collectivist or communist anarchism" because this was the kind of anarchism which had most in common with Marxism.[73]

The reason Guérin gave for focussing on this kind of anarchism, as opposed to insurrectionist, individualist or illegalist anarchism or terrorism, was that it was entirely relevant to the problems faced by contemporary revolutionaries: "libertarian visions of the future . . . invite serious consideration. It is clear that they fulfil to a very large extent the needs of our times, and that they can contribute to the building of our future."[74]

But is this really "classical anarchism," as Guérin put it, given the insistence on "constructive anarchism, which depends on organisation, on self-discipline, on integration, on federalist and noncoercive centralisation"; the emphasis on experiments in workers' control in Algeria, Yugoslavia and Cuba; the openness to the idea that such states could be seen as socialist and capable of reform in a libertarian direction?[75] This was not the conclusion of English anarchist Nicolas Walter, whose review of *Ni dieu ni maître* commented that "the selection of passages shows a consistent bias towards activism, and the more intellectual, theoretical and philosophical approach to anarchism is almost completely ignored. . . . There is a similar bias towards revolution, and the more moderate, pragmatic and reformist approach to anarchism is almost completely omitted as well."[76] As for Guérin's *L'Anarchisme*, Walter detected a similar bias towards Proudhon and Bakunin, and was surprised at the emphasis on Gramsci, "which might be expected in a Marxist account [of the Italian workers' councils after the Great War] but is refreshing in an anarchist one." Walter was also sceptical about the attention paid to Algeria and Yugoslavia. In summary, however, these two books were "the expression of an original and exciting view of anarchism."[77]

So Guérin's two books arguably represented an original departure, and it is worth quoting some remarks made by Patrice Spadoni who worked alongside Guérin in different libertarian communist groups in the 1970s and 1980s:

> It has to be said that Daniel Guérin's non-dogmatism never ceased to amaze us. In the 1970s, a period in which there was so much blinkeredness and sectarianism, in our own ranks as well as among the Leninists, Daniel would often take us aback. The young libertarian communists that we were . . .turned pale with shock when he sang the praises of a Proudhon, of whom he was saying "yes and no" while we said "no and no"; then we would go white with horror, when he started quoting Stirner whom we loathed—without having really read him; then we became livid, when he began a dialogue with social-democrats; and finally, we practically had a melt-down when he expressed respect, albeit without agreeing with them, for the revolt of the militants associated with *Action directe*.[78]

Two of these taboos are worth picking up on when considering the extent to which Guérin's take on anarchism was a novel one: Proudhon and Stirner.

Proudhon and the Fundamental Importance of Self-management

Proudhon had already ceased to be an ideological reference for any section of the French anarchist movement by at least the time of the Great War, except for a small minority of individualists opposed to any kind of collective ownership of the means of production. Most anarchists referred to either Kropotkin or Bakunin. This was partly because of the ambiguities in Proudhon's own writings regarding property, and partly because of the increasingly reactionary positions adopted by some of his "Mutualist" followers after his death in 1865.

The fact that Proudhon is so central to Guérin's "rehabilitation" of anarchism is thus surprising and tells us something about what he was trying to do and how it is he came to study anarchism in such depth: whereas Proudhon had already for many years been commonly referred to as the "père de l'anarchie," the "father of anarchy," Guérin refers to him as the "père de l'autogestion," the "father of self-management." This is the crux of the matter: Guérin was looking for a way to guarantee that in any future revolution, control of the workplace, of the economy and of society as a whole would remain at the base, that spontaneous forms of democracy—like the soviets, in the beginning—would not be hijacked by any centralised power.[79] Marx, Guérin insisted, hardly mentioned workers' control or self-management at all, whereas Proudhon paid it a great deal of attention.[80] Workers' control was, for Guérin, "without any doubt the most original creation of anarchism, and goes right to the heart of contemporary realities."[81] Proudhon had been one of the first to try to answer the question raised by other social reformers of the early nineteenth century. As Guérin put it: "Who should manage the economy? Private capitalism? The state? Workers' organisations? In other words, there were—and still are—three options: free enterprise, nationalisation, or socialisation (i.e., self-management)."[82] From 1840 onwards, Proudhon had argued passionately for the third option, something which set him apart from most other socialists of the time, who, like Louis Blanc, argued for one form or another of state control (if only on a transitional basis). Unlike Marx, Engels and others, Guérin argued, Proudhon saw workers' control as a concrete problem to be raised now, rather than relegated to some distant future. As a consequence, he thought and wrote in detail about how it might function: "Almost all the issues which have caused such problems for present-day experiments in self-management were already foreseen and described in Proudhon's writings."[83]

Stirner the "Father of Anarchism"?

As for Stirner—generally anathema to the non-individualist wing of the anarchist movement—the answer lies in what Guérin perceived to be Stirner's latent homosexuality, his concern with sexual liberation and his determination to attack bourgeois prejudice and puritanism: "Stirner was a precursor of May '68."[84] His "greatest claim to originality, his most memorable idea, was his discovery of the "unique" individual. . . . Stirner became, as a consequence, the voice of all those who throw down a challenge to normality."[85]

What we can see here, underlying Guérin's approving summary of the meaning and importance of Stirner, is someone who had for many years been forced to suffer in silence because of the endemic homophobia of the labour movement, someone who had been forced by society's moral prejudices to live a near-schizoid existence, totally suppressing one half of his personality. It was Guérin's personal experience of and outrage at the homophobia of many Marxists and what seemed to be classical Marxism's exclusive concern with materialism and class that accounts in large part for his sympathy with Stirner.

So to the extent that Guérin insists that every anarchist is an individualist—at the same time as being a "social" anarchist (*anarchiste sociétaire*)—to the extent that he approves of Stirner's emphasis on the uniqueness of each individual, it is because he admires the determination to resist social conformism and moral prejudice. Guérin certainly had no truck with the precious "freedom of the individual" which by the 1920s had already become the stock mantra of those anarchists who rejected any attempt to produce a more ideologically and organisationally coherent revolutionary movement or who wished to ground their action in a realistic (or in Guérin's words "scientific") analysis of social conditions.

For a "Synthesis" of Marxism and Anarchism

So having called himself a "libertarian socialist" in the late 1950s before going through an "anarchist phase" in the 1960s, by 1968 Guérin was advocating "libertarian Marxism," a term he would later change to "libertarian communism" in order not to alienate some of his new anarchist friends (though the content remained the same). In 1969, with Georges Fontenis and others Guérin launched the *Mouvement communiste libertaire* (MCL), which attempted to bring together various groups such as supporters of Denis Berger's *Voie communiste*, former members of the FCL and individuals such as Gabriel Cohn-Bendit who had been associated with Socialisme ou Barbarie.[86] Guérin was responsible for the organisation's paper, *Guerre de classes* (*Class War*). In 1971, the MCL merged with another group to become the *Organisation communiste libertaire* (OCL). In 1980, after complex debates notably over the question of trade union activity, Guérin—who rejected ultra-Left forms of "*spontanéisme*" which condemned trade unionism as counter-revolutionary— would ultimately join the *Union des travailleurs communistes libertaires* (UTCL), created in 1978. He would remain a member until his death in 1988.[87]

Looking back on those years, Georges Fontenis would write: "For us [the FCL], as for Guérin, 'libertarian Marxism' was never to be seen as a fusion or a marriage, but as a living synthesis very different from the sum of its parts."[88] How should we interpret this?

Guérin was always keen to emphasise the commonalities in Marxism and anarchism, and underscored the fact that, in his view at least, they shared the same roots and the same objectives. Having said that, and despite the fact that Rubel seems to have influenced Guérin, Guérin's study of Marx led him to suggest that those such as Rubel who saw Marx as a libertarian were exaggerating and/or being too selective.[89] Reviewing the ambivalent but predominantly hostile relations between Marx and Engels, on the one hand, and Stirner, Proudhon, and Bakunin, on the other, Guérin concluded that the disagreements between them were based to a great extent on misunderstanding and exaggeration on both sides: "Each of the two movements needs the theoretical and practical contribution of the other," Guérin argued, and this is why he saw the expulsion of the Bakuninists from the International Working Men's Association Congress at The Hague in 1872 as "a disastrous event for the working class."[90]

"Libertarian communism" was for Guérin an attempt to "revivify everything that was constructive in anarchism's contribution in the past." We have noted that his *Anarchism* focused on "social, constructive, collectivist, or communist anarchism."[91] Guérin was more critical of "traditional" anarchism, with what he saw as its knee-jerk rejection of organisation, and particularly what he considered to be its Manichean and simplistic approach to the question of the "state" in modern, industrial and increasingly internationalised societies. He became interested particularly in militants such as the Spanish anarchist Diego Abad de Santillán, whose ideas on "integrated" economic self-management contrasted with what Guérin insisted was the naive and backward-looking "libertarian communism" of the Spanish CNT advocated at its 1936 Saragossa conference by Isaac Puente and inspired, Guérin thought, by Kropotkin.[92] Such a policy seemed to Guérin to take no account of the nature of modern consumer societies and the need for economic planning and coordination at national and transnational level. In this connection, Guérin also became interested in the ideas of the Belgian collectivist socialist César de Paepe—who argued against the anarchists of the Jura Federation in favour of what he called an "an-archic state"—on the national and transnational organisation of public services within a libertarian framework.[93]

On the other hand, Guérin's libertarian Marxism or communism did not reject those aspects of Marxism which still seemed to Guérin valid and useful: (i) the notion of alienation, much discussed since Erich Fromm's 1941 *Fear of Freedom*, and which Guérin saw as being in accordance with the anarchist emphasis on the freedom and autonomy of the individual; (ii) the insistence that the workers shall be emancipated by the workers themselves; (iii) the analysis of capitalist society; and (iv) the historical materialist dialectic, which for Guérin remained

> one of the guiding threads enabling us to understand the past
> and the present, on condition that the method not be applied
> rigidly, mechanically, or as an excuse not to fight on the false

pretext that the material conditions for a revolution are absent, as the Stalinists claimed was the case in France in 1936, 1945 and 1968. Historical materialism must never be reduced to a determinism; the door must always be open to individual will and to the revolutionary spontaneity of the masses.[94]

Indeed, following his focus on anarchism in the 1960s, Guérin returned in the 1970s to his earlier researches on Marxism, and in his new quest for a synthesis of the two ideologies he found a particularly fruitful source in Rosa Luxemburg, in whom he developed a particular interest and he played a role in the wider resurgence of interest in her ideas. She was for Guérin the only German social democrat who stayed true to what he called "original" Marxism, and in 1971 he published an anthology of her critical writings on the pre-1914 SFIO, as well as an important study of the notion of spontaneity in her work.[95] Guérin saw no significant difference between her conception of revolutionary working-class spontaneity and the anarchist one, nor between her conception of the "mass strike" and the syndicalist idea of the "general strike." Her criticisms of Lenin in 1904 and of the Bolshevik Party in the spring of 1918 (regarding the democratic freedoms of the working class) seemed to him very anarchistic, as did her conception of a socialism propelled from below by workers' councils. She was, he argued, "one of the links between anarchism and authentic Marxism," and for this reason she played an important role in the development of Guérin's thinking about convergences between certain forms of Marxism and certain forms of anarchism.[96]

Guérin was convinced that a libertarian communism which represented such a synthesis of the best of Marxism and the best of anarchism would be much more attractive to progressive workers than "degenerate, authoritarian Marxism or old, outdated, and fossilised anarchism."[97] But he was adamant that he was not a theorist, that libertarian communism was, as yet, only an "approximation," not a fixed dogma:

It cannot, it seems to me, be defined on paper, in absolute terms. It cannot be an endless raking over of the past, but must rather be a rallying point for the future. The only thing of which I am convinced is that the future social revolution will have nothing to do with either Muscovite despotism or anæmic social-democracy; that it will not be authoritarian, but libertarian and rooted in self-management, or, if you like, councilist.[98]

Conclusion

To what extent, then, can we say that Guérin succeeded in producing a "synthesis"? Assessments by fellow revolutionaries have varied. Guérin himself used to complain that many militants were so attached to ideological pigeonholing and that quasi-tribal loyalties were so strong that his purpose was frequently misunderstood, with many who identified as anarchists criticising him for having "become a Marxist," and vice versa.[99] Yet Guérin was always very clear that there have been many different Marxisms and many different anarchisms, and he also insisted that his understanding of "libertarian communism" went beyond or transcended ("*dépasse*") both anarchism and Marxism.[100]

Nicolas Walter, in a broadly positive review of Guérin's work, and apparently struggling to characterise his politics, described him as "a veteran socialist who became an anarchist" and as "a Marxist writer of a more or less Trotskyist variety" who had gone on to attempt a synthesis between Marxism and anarchism before finally turning to "a syndicalist form of anarchism."[101]

George Woodcock, in a review of Noam Chomsky's introduction to the Monthly Review Press edition of Guérin's *Anarchism*, insisted that "neither is an anarchist by any known criterion; they are both left-wing Marxists"—their failing having been to focus too narrowly on the economic, on workers' control, on an "obsolete," "anarcho-syndicalist" perspective.[102] Such a judgement is clearly based on a particular and not uncontentious conception of anarchism.

The opposite conclusion was drawn by another anarchist, Miguel Chueca, who has argued that if we look at all the major issues dividing anarchists from Marxists—namely, according to Guérin's *Pour un Marxisme libertaire*, the post-revolutionary "withering away" of the state, the role of minorities (or vanguards or avant-gardes) and the resort to bourgeois democratic methods—then "the 'synthesis' results, in all cases, in a choice in favour of the anarchist position."[103] Chueca seems to have based his conclusion on an essentialist view of anarchism (in the singular) and of Marxism, and on an identification of Marxism with Leninism. He appears to disregard some significant issues, such as Guérin's insistence on the historical materialist dialectic, and the need for centralised (albeit "non-coercive") economic planning.

Writing from a sympathetic but not uncritical, Trotskyist perspective, Ian Birchall suggests that ultimately Guérin's greatest achievement was his practice as a militant:

Guérin's greatness lay in his role as a mediator rather than as a synthesist. Over six decades he had a record of willingness to cooperate with any section of the French left that shared his fundamental goals of proletarian self-emancipation, colonial liberation and sexual freedom. He was a vigorous polemicist, but saw no fragment of the left, however obscure, as beneath his attention. . . . He was also typically generous, never seeking to malign his opponents, however profoundly he disagreed with them. . . . He was always willing to challenge orthodoxy, whether Marxist or anarchist. . . . Yet behind the varying formulations one consistent principle remained: "The Revolution of our age will be made from below—or not at all."[104]

Others have embraced Guérin's theoretical contribution and it is clear that his ideas on a "libertarian Marxism" or "libertarian communism" were enormously influential from the 1960s onwards, and many today (notably, but not only, those in France close to the organisation *Alternative libertaire*[105]) see in him a precursor and are admiring of his theoretical and practical contribution to the search for a libertarian communism—albeit as a contribution which needed further development in the context of the social struggles of the 1980s and beyond. Indeed Guérin was the first to accept that he had not yet seen the "definitive crystalisation of such an unconventional and difficult synthesis," which would "emerge from social struggles" with "innovative forms which nobody today can claim to predict"[106]:

It would be pointless today to try to paper over the cracks in the more or less crumbling and rotting edifice of socialist doctrines, to plug away at patching together some of those fragments of traditional Marxism and anarchism which are still useful, to launch oneself into demonstrations of Marxian or Bakuninian erudition, to attempt to trace, merely on paper, ingenious syntheses or tortuous reconciliations. . . . To call oneself a libertarian communist today, does not mean looking backwards, but towards the future. The libertarian communist is not an exegete, but a militant.[107]

Notes

1. Daniel Guérin, *Front populaire, Révolution manquée. Témoignage militant* (Arles: Editions Actes Sud, 1977), p. 29. All translations in this introduction are the present author's, unless stated otherwise.

2. In *Questions de méthode*, quoted in Ian Birchall, 'Sartre's Encounter with Daniel Guérin', *Sartre Studies International* vol. 2, no. 1 (1996), p. 46.

3. See Louis Janover, 'Daniel Guérin, le trouble-fête' in *L'Homme et la société* no. 94 (1989), thematic issue on 'Dissonances dans la Révolution', pp. 83–93.

4. Letter to Marceau Pivert, 18 November 1947, Bibliothèque de Documentation Internationale Contemporaine (hereafter BDIC), Fonds Guérin, F°Δ Rés 688/10/2. *La Lutte de classes sous la Première République, 1793–1797* [Class Struggle under the First Republic] (Paris: Gallimard, 1946; new edition 1968), 2 vols.

5. Alex Callinicos (ed.), *Marxist Theory* (Oxford University Press, 1989), p. 108.

6. Daniel Guérin, À *la recherche d'un communisme libertaire* (Paris: Spartacus, 1984), pp. 10–1.

7. See D. Berry, 'Metamorphosis: The Making of Daniel Guérin, 1904–1930' in *Modern & Contemporary France* vol. 22, no. 3 (2014), pp. 321–42, and 'From Son of the Bourgeoisie to Servant of the Revolution: The Roots of Daniel Guérin's Revolutionary Socialism' in *Moving the Social—Journal of Social History and the History of Social Movements* no. 51 (2014), pp. 283–311.

8. On Malon, see K. Steven Vincent, *Between Marxism and Anarchism: Benoît Malon and French Reformist Socialism* (Berkeley: University of California Press, 1992). On Proudhon and Kropotkin, see Iain McKay's edited anthologies, both of which have useful introductions: *Property Is Theft! A Pierre-Joseph Proudhon Reader* (Oakland: AK Press, 2011) and *Direct Struggle Against Capital: A Peter Kropotkin Anthology* (Oakland: AK Press, 2014).

9. Cf. Alexandre Christoyannopoulos, 'Leo Tolstoy on the State: A Detailed Picture of Tolstoy's Denunciation of State Violence and Deception', in *Anarchist Studies* vol. 16, no. 1 (Spring 2008), pp. 20–47.

10. Daniel Guérin, *Autobiographie de jeunesse, d'une dissidence sexuelle au socialisme* (Paris: Belfond, 1972), pp. 126–7. Charles Maurras was the leader of the right-wing, nationalist and royalist movement, *Action Française*.

11. For more detail, see D. Berry, '"Workers of the World, Embrace!" Daniel Guérin, the Labour Movement and Homosexuality' in *Left History* vol. 9, no. 2 (Spring/Summer 2004), pp. 11–43. See also Peter Sedgwick, 'Out of Hiding: The Comradeships of Daniel Guérin', *Salmagundi* vol. 58, no. 9 (June 1982), pp. 197–220.

12. Guérin, À la recherche, p. 9; Guérin, *Front populaire*, p. 23.

13. Guérin, *Front populaire*, p. 147.

14. See Thierry Hohl, 'Daniel Guérin, 'pivertiste'. Un parcours dans la Gauche révolutionnaire de la SFIO (1935–1938)' in *Dissidences* 2 (2007), pp. 133–49, and Jacques Kergoat, *Marceau Pivert, 'socialiste de gauche'* (Paris: Les Editions de l'Atelier/Editions Ouvrières, 1994). '*Luxembourgisme*' was an identifiable current on the French left opposed to both Bolshevism and social democracy from around 1928–31. See Alain Guillerm's preface to the third edition of Rosa Luxembourg, *Marxisme et Dictature: La démocratie selon Lénine et Luxembourg* (Paris: Spartacus, 1974).

15. Guérin's *Front populaire* is a classic 'revolutionist' interpretation of the Popular Front experience.

16. What has since become known as 'entryism' ('entrisme' in French) was originally referred to as 'the French turn' ('le tournant français'). This was the new tactic proposed by Trotsky in 1934 in response to the growing fascist threat across Europe, and the first instance of it was the suggestion in June of that year that the French Trotskyists enter the PS in order to contribute to the development of a more radical current within the party. See Daniel Bensaïd, *Les trotskysmes* (Paris: Presses Universitaires de France, 2002), pp. 31–2 and Alex Callinicos, *Trotskyism* (Minneapolis: University of Minnesota Press, 1990), pp. 18–9.

17. Guérin, *Front populaire*, p. 104. Guérin's *Fascisme et grand capital* (Paris: Gallimard, 1936) was inspired by Trotsky.

18. Guérin, *La Peste brune a passé par là* (Paris: Librairie du Travail, 1933), translated as *The Brown Plague: Travels in Late Weimar and Early Nazi Germany* (Durham, NC: Duke University Press, 1994); *Fascisme et grand capital* (Paris: Gallimard, 1936), trans. *Fascism and Big Business* (New York: Monad Press, 1973). *Fascism* has been criticised by some for tending towards reductionism: see Claude Lefort, 'L'analyse Marxiste et le fascisme', *Les Temps modernes* 2 (November 1945), pp. 357–62. Guérin defended himself vigorously against such criticisms, and many regard his analysis as fundamentally correct: see for example Alain Bihr's introduction to the 1999 edition of *Fascisme et grand capital* (Paris: Editions Syllepse and Phénix Editions), pp. 7–14.

19. Guérin, 'Quand le fascisme nous devançait', in *La Peste brune* (Paris: Spartacus, 1996), pp. 21–2.

20. Ibid., p. 25.

21. Guérin, *Front populaire*, pp. 150, 156–7, 365.

22. Ibid., p. 157.

23. Ibid., p. 213.

24. Ibid., p. 23.

25. See Jean van Heijenoort, 'Manifeste: La France sous Hitler et Pétain', in Rodolphe Prager (ed.), *Les congrès de la quatrième internationale (manifestes, thèses, résolutions)* (Paris: La Brèche, 1981) vol. II, pp. 35–44; L. Trotsky, 'La guerre impérialiste et la révolution prolétarienne mondiale' in D. Guérin (ed.), *Sur la deuxième guerre mondiale* (Brussels: Editions la Taupe, 1970), pp. 187–245. An English-language version of the manifesto is available on the Marxists Internet Archive at https://www.marxists.org/history/etol/document/fi/1938-1949/emergconf/fi-emerg02.htm.

26. Interview with Pierre André Boutang in *Guérin*, television documentary by Jean-José Marchand (1985; broadcast on FR3, 4 & 11 September 1989). For more details, see D. Berry, '"Like a Wisp of Straw Amidst the Raging Elements": Daniel Guérin in the Second World War', in Hanna Diamond and Simon Kitson (eds.), *Vichy, Resistance, Liberation: New Perspectives on Wartime France (Festschrift in Honour of H.R. Kedward)* (Oxford: Berg, 2005), pp. 143–54.

27. Letter to Marceau Pivert, 2 Januaury 1948, BDIC, Fonds Guérin, F°Δ Rés 688/9/1.

28. Daniel Guérin, *Le Feu du Sang. Autobiographie politique et charnelle* (Paris: Editions Grasset & Fasquelle, 1977), p. 149. On Guérin's tour of the U.S., see ibid., pp. 143–219. Guérin's researches led to the publication of the two-volume *Où va le peuple américain?* (Paris: Julliard, 1950–51). Sections of this would be published separately as *Décolonisation du Noir américain* (Paris: Minuit, 1963), *Le Mouvement ouvrier aux États-Unis* (Paris: Maspero, 1968), *La concentration économique aux États-Unis* (Paris: Anthropos, 1971)—which included a 33pp. preface by the Trotskyist economist Ernest Mandel—and *De l'Oncle Tom aux Panthères: Le drame des Noirs américains* (Paris: UGE, 1973). Translations: *Negroes on the March: A Frenchman's Report on the American Negro Struggle*, trans. Duncan Ferguson (New York: George L. Weissman, 1956), and *100 Years of Labour in the USA*, trans. Alan Adler (London: Ink Links, 1979). For a discussion of Guérin's analysis, see also Larry Portis, 'Daniel Guérin et les États-Unis: l'optimisme et l'intelligence' in *Agone* 29–30 (2003), pp. 277–89.

29. Guérin, *La Lutte de classes sous la Pemière République, 1793–1797*, 2 vols. (Paris: Gallimard, 1946; 2nd edition 1968). See also Denis Berger, 'La révolution plurielle (pour Daniel Guérin)' in E. Balibar, J.-S. Beek, D. Bensaïd et al., *Permanences de la Révolution. Pour un autre bicentenaire* (Paris: La Brèche, 1989), pp. 195–208; David Berry, 'Daniel Guérin à la Libération. De l'historien de la Révolution au militant révolutionnaire: un tournant

idéologique', *Agone* 29–30 (2003), pp. 257–73; Michel Lequenne, 'Daniel Guérin, l'homme de 93 et le problème de Robespierre', *Critique communiste* 130–1 (May 1993), pp. 31–4; Julia Guseva, 'La Terreur pendant la Révolution et l'interprétation de D. Guérin', *Dissidences* 2 (2007), pp. 77–88; Jean-Numa Ducange, 'Comment Daniel Guérin utilise-t-il l'œuvre de Karl Kautsky sur la Révolution française dans *La Lutte de classes sous la première République*, et pourquoi?', ibid., pp. 89–111. Norah Carlin, 'Daniel Guérin and the working class in the French Revolution', *International Socialism* 47 (1990), pp. 197–223, discusses changes made by Guérin to *La Lutte de classes* for the 1968 edition.

30. Guérin, *La Révolution française et nous* (Paris: Maspero, 1976), pp. 7–8. Note that the reference to 'libertarian socialism' is in the preface to *La Révolution française et nous*, written thirty years after the main text and after Guérin had moved closer to anarchism.

31. Cf. Murray Bookchin's comments on the *sections* in 'The Forms of Freedom' (1968) in *Post-Scarcity Anarchism* (Montréal: Black Rose Books, 1971), p. 165.

32. Guérin, *La Lutte de classes* (1968), vol. I, p. 31.

33. Ibid., p. 58.

34. E.J. Hobsbawm, *Echoes of the Marseillaise: Two Centuries Look Back on the French Revolution* (London: Verso, 1990), p. 53.

35. Guérin, *La Révolution française et nous*, p. 7.

36. For an overview, see Olivier Bétourné and Aglaia I. Hartig, *Penser l'histoire de la Révolution. Deux siècles de passion française* (Paris: La Découverte, 1989), esp. pp. 110–4. For a recent reassessment of the long-running dispute between Guérin and G. Lefebvre, see Antonio de Francesco, 'Daniel Guérin et Georges Lefebvre, une rencontre improbable', *La Révolution française*, http://lrf.revues.org/index162.html, date accessed 28 March 2011.

37. Ian Birchall, 'Sartre's Encounter with Daniel Guérin', *Sartre Studies International* vol. 2, no. 1 (1996), p. 46.

38. Guérin, 'Faisons le point', *Le Libérateur politique et social pour la nouvelle gauche* (12 February 1956). A populist, reactionary and xenophobic anti-taxation movement of small shopkeepers, founded by Pierre Poujade in 1953, 'Poujadisme' had "more than a hint of fascism" as Rod Kedward has put it—see *La Vie en Bleu. France and the French since 1900* (London: Penguin, 2006), p. 376. It was as a representative of Poujade's party that Jean-Marie Le Pen was elected to the National Assembly in 1956.

39. C.L.R. James, 'L'actualité de la Révolution française', *Perspectives socialistes: Revue bimensuelle de l'Union de la Gauche Socialiste* 4 (15 February 1958), pp. 20–1.

40. Guérin, 'La Révolution déjacobinisée', in *Jeunesse du socialisme libertaire* (Paris: Rivière, 1959), pp. 27–63. See 'The French Revolution De-Jacobinized' in the present collection.

41. *La Révolution française et nous* was originally intended as the preface to *La Lutte de classes*. 'Quand le fascisme nous devançait' was originally commissioned for a special issue of *Les Temps Modernes* on the state of the left, but

was then rejected by Sartre for being too critical of the PCF, according to a letter from Guérin to C.L.R. James, 10 August 1955, BDIC, Fonds Guérin, F°Δ 721/60/5.

42. Guérin, 'La Révolution déjacobinisée', p. 43.

43. Ibid., pp. 43–4.

44. Guérin, 'Preface', in *Jeunesse du socialisme libertaire*, pp. 7–8.

45. Guérin, 'La Révolution déjacobinisée', 30–1.

46. Michel Crozier, *Ma Belle Epoque. Mémoires. 1947–1969* (Paris: Fayard, 2002), pp. 79 & 86.

47. Guérin, *Le Feu du sang*, p. 218; Kent Worcester, *C.L.R. James. A Political Biography* (Albany: SUNY, 1996), p. 201; James, letter to Guérin, 24 May 1956, BDIC, Fonds Guérin, F°Δ 721/57/2.

48. Guérin, *Le Feu du sang*, p. 189. In his account of these meetings, Guérin refers positively to the collection *La Contre-révolution bureaucratique* (Paris: UGE, 1973), which contained texts by Korsch, Pannekoek, Rühle and others taken from *International Council Correspondence, Living Marxism* and *International Socialism*. The councilists had previously republished in translation an article of Guérin's from the French syndicalist journal *Révolution prolétarienne*: 'Fascist Corporatism', in *International Council Correspondence* vol. 3, no. 2 (February 1937), pp. 14–26. (I am grateful to Saku Pinta for bringing this to my attention.) On Korsch, see Douglas Kellner (ed.), *Karl Korsch: Revolutionary Theory* (Austin: University of Texas Press, 1977), which includes a lengthy biographical study.

49. Guérin/Korsch correspondence, April–June 1954, Karl Korsch Papers, Internationaal Instituut voor Sociale Geschiedenis (hereafter IISG), Boxes 1–24.

50. Guérin, *Le Feu du sang*, p. 156.

51. Guérin Papers, IISG, Box 1, Folder 14. Pierre Chaulieu and Claude Montal were the pseudonyms of Cornelius Castoriadis and Claude Lefort respectively.

52. The list also included James Guillaume's history of the IWMA, Victor Serge's *Memoirs of a Revolutionary*, Voline's *The Unknown Revolution*, Makhno, and the many publications of the Spartacus group created by René Lefeuvre. Mohammed Harbi, *Une Vie debout. Mémoires politiques, Tome I: 1945–1962* (Paris: La Découverte, 2001), pp. 109–12. Harbi incorrectly describes the Cercle Lénine as being connected to the PCF; see *La Vérité*, 1 January 1954. On the different analyses of the nature of the USSR, see Marcel van der Linden, *Western Marxism and the Soviet Union. A Survey of Critical Theories and Debates Since 1917* (Chicago: Haymarket Books, 2007); on Castoriadis and Lefort, see pp. 116–8.

53. Edgar Morin, 'L'Anarchisme en 1968', *Magazine littéraire* 19 (1968), available at www.magazine-litteraire.com/archives/ar_anar.htm, accessed 6 October 2002.

54. See Edgar Morin, 'La réfome de pensée', in *Arguments, 1956–1962* (Toulouse: Privat, 1983), vol. I, p. ix.

55. For an explanation of why Yugoslavia's break with the Soviet bloc in 1948 was so important to the extreme left in the west, see the semi-autobiographical account in chapter 5, 'Les "années yougoslaves"', of *Le Trotskisme. Une histoire sans fard* (Paris: Editions Syllepse, 2005) by Guérin's friend and comrade Michel Lequenne.

56. Anne Guérin, 'Les ruptures de Daniel Guérin. Notice biographique', in Daniel Guérin, *De l'Oncle Tom aux Panthères noires* (Pantin: Les bons caractères, 2010), p. 9.

57. On the FCL, see Georges Fontenis, *Changer le monde: Histoire du mouvement communiste libertaire, 1945–1997* (Paris: Alternative libertaire, 2000) and, for a more critical view, Philippe Dubacq, *Anarchisme et Marxisme au travers de la Fédération communiste libertaire (1945–1956)*, Noir et Rouge 23 (1991).

58. Guérin, *Le Feu du sang*, p. 233.

59. Guérin, *À la recherche*, p. 9.

60. Ibid., p. 9.

61. Ibid., p. 10. *L'Anarchisme, de la doctrine à la pratique* (Paris: Gallimard, 1965); *Ni Dieu ni Maître, anthologie de l'anarchisme* (Lausanne: La Cité-Lausanne, 1965). Both have been republished several times since, and *L'Anarchisme* has been translated into more than 20 languages. They have been published in English as *Anarchism: From Theory to Practice* (New York: Monthly Review Press, 1970), with an introduction by Noam Chomsky, and *No Gods No Masters: An Anthology of Anarchism* (Edinburgh: AK Press, 1998).

62. This is not uncontentious—indeed Ernest Mandel takes issue with Guérin over this question in his anthology *Contrôle ouvrier, conseils ouvriers, autogestion* (Paris: Maspero, 1970), p. 7.

63. See Guérin's 1969 article, 'Conseils ouvriers et syndicalisme révolutionnaire. L'exemple hongrois, 1956' in À la recherche, pp. 111–5; the same piece was republished as 'Syndicalisme révolutionnaire et conseillisme' in *Pour le communisme libertaire*, pp. 155–62.

64. Letters to the author, 12 and 26 February 1986. *L'en dehors* appeared weekly, 1922–39, and used to campaign for complete sexual freedom, regarding homosexuality as an entirely valid form of 'free love'. See Richard D. Sonn, *Sex, Violence, and the Avant-Garde: Anarchism in Interwar France* (University Park: Pennsylvania State University Press, 2010).

65. Georges Fontenis, 'Le long parcours de Daniel Guérin vers le communisme libertaire', special number of *Alternative Libertaire* on Guérin (1998), p. 37.

66. Guérin, *Le Feu du sang*, p. 228.

67. It is also noteworthy that Guérin would include a section on decolonisation in his *Anarchism* and found material from Proudhon and Bakunin which supported the FCL's position. See Sylvain Pattieu, *Les camarades des frères: Trotskistes et libertaires dans la guerre d'Algérie* (Paris: Syllepse, 2002); Sidi Mohammed Barkat (ed.), *Des Français contre la terreur d'Etat (Algérie 1954–1962)* (Paris: Editions Reflex, 2002); Sylvain Boulouque, *Les anarchistes français face aux guerres coloniales (1945–1962)* (Lyon: Atelier de création libertaire, 2003).

68.   According to a note by the editors in Guérin, *Pour le communisme libertaire* (Paris: Spartacus, 2003), p. 5. Rubel (1905–96) had had links with the councilist movement and would publish the short text, 'Marx théoricien de l'anarchisme' [Marx, theoretician of anarchism] in his *Marx, critique du Marxisme* [Marx, critic of Marxism] (Paris: Editions Payot, 1974; new edition 2000), a collection of articles previously published between 1957 and 1973. The text has since been published as a booklet, *Marx théoricien de l'anarchisme* (Saint-Denis: Vent du ch'min, 1983; Geneva: Editions Entremonde, 2010). His argument in brief was that 'under the name communism, Marx developed a theory of anarchism; and further, that in fact it was he who was the first to provide a rational basis for the anarchist utopia and to put forward a project for achieving it.' Marxists Internet Archive, www.Marxists.org/archive/rubel/1973/marx-anarchism.htm, accessed 29 March 2011.

69.   Preface of 1970 to Guérin (ed.), *Ni Dieu ni Maître. Anthologie de l'anarchisme* (Paris: La Découverte, 1999), vol. I, pp. 6–7. See pp. 41–3 in this volume.

70.   *L'Anarchisme*, p. 21.

71.   Daniel Guérin, *Pour un Marxisme libertaire* (Paris: Robert Laffont, 1969), p. 7.

72.   Georges Fontenis, 'Le long parcours', p. 38.

73.   'Anarchisme et Marxisme', p. 237, in *L'Anarchisme* (1981 edition), pp. 229–52. For an English-language version, see the booklet *Anarchism & Marxism* (Sanday, Orkney: Cienfuegos Press, 1981), or 'Marxism and Anarchism', in David Goodway (ed.), *For Anarchism: History, Theory and Practice* (London: Routledge, 1989), pp. 109–26.

74.   *L'Anarchisme*, pp. 13–4.

75.   *Anarchism*, p. 153.

76.   Nicolas Walter, 'Daniel Guerin's Anarchism', *Anarchy* vol. 8, no. 94 (1968), p. 378.

77.   Ibid., p. 381.

78.   Patrice Spadoni, 'La synthèse entre l'anarchisme et le Marxisme: "Un point de ralliement vers l'avenir"', *Alternative Libertaire* special number (2000), p. 43. Guérin, *Proudhon oui et non* (Paris: Gallimard, 1978),

79.   See his '1917–1921, de l'autogestion à la bureaucratie soviétique', in *De la Révolution d'octobre à l'empire éclaté: 70 ans de réflexions sur la nature de l'URSS* (Paris: Alternative libertaire/UTCL, n.d.); 'Proudhon et l'autogestion ouvrière' in *L'Actualité de Proudhon* (Bruxelles: Université libre de Bruxelles, 1967), pp. 67–87; 'L'Espagne libertaire', editorial introduction to part of *Autogestion et socialisme*, special issue on 'Les anarchistes et l'autogestion' nos. 18/19 (janvier–avril 1972), pp. 81–2; 'L'autogestion contemporaine', *Noir et rouge* nos. 31/32 (octobre 1965–février 1966), pp. 16–24.

80.   See similarly critical remarks about Marxism's neglect of this issue by Castoriadis in an interview for a special issue of the UTCL's magazine on the usefulness (or otherwise) of Marxism for libertarian communists: 'Marx aujourd'hui. Entretien avec Cornelius Castoriadis' *Lutter!* no. 5 (May 1983), pp. 15–8. Guérin's article on 'Marx et Engels militants' appeared in the same issue, pp. 19–20.

81. *L'Anarchisme*, p. 16.
82. 'Proudhon père de l'autogestion' (1965) in *Proudhon oui et non* (Paris: Gallimard, 1978), p. 165.
83. Ibid., p. 191.
84. Guérin, *Ni Dieu ni Maître*, vol. I, p. 12. Guérin began his anthology of anarchist texts with the 'precursor' Stirner; he also added an appendix on Stirner to the 1981 edition of *L'Anarchisme*. See also D. Guérin, *Homosexualité et Révolution* (Saint-Denis: Le Vent du ch'min, 1983), p. 12, and 'Stirner, "Père de l'anarchisme"?', *La Rue* 26 (1er et 2ème trimestre 1979), pp. 76–89. Guérin also believed Proudhon to have been a repressed homosexual: see 'Proudhon et l'amour "unisexual"' in *Arcadie* nos. 133/134 (janvier/février 1965).
85. 'Stirner, "Père de l'anarchisme"?', p. 83.
86. See Fontenis, *Changer le monde*, pp. 161–2 and 255–6.
87. The UTCL's manifesto, adopted at its Fourth Congress in 1986, was republished (with a dedication to Guérin) by the UTCL's successor organisation, Alternative Libertaire: *Un projet de société communiste libertaire* (Paris: Alternative libertaire, 2002). See also Théo Rival, *Syndicalistes et libertaires: Une histoire de l'Union des travailleurs communistes libertaires (1974–1991)* (Paris: Editions d'Alternative libertaire, 2013).
88. Fontenis, *Changer le monde*, p. 80, note 1. See also David Berry, 'Change the world without taking power? The libertarian communist tradition in France today', *Journal of Contemporary European Studies* vol. 16, no. 1 (Spring 2008), pp. 111–30.
89. Guérin, 'Anarchisme et Marxisme', in *L'Anarchisme* (1981), p. 250.
90. Ibid., p. 248.
91. Ibid., p. 237.
92. On Abad de Santillán, see the section on 'L'Espagne libertaire', in *Les anarchistes et l'autogestion*, special issue on 'Autogestion et socialisme' nos. 18–19 (1972), pp. 81–117, including an introduction by Guérin.
93. See Guérin, *Ni Dieu ni Maître*, vol. I, pp. 268–91.
94. Guérin, 'Anarchisme et Marxisme', in *L'Anarchisme* (1981), p. 252.
95. Rosa Luxemburg, *Le socialisme en France, 1898–1912* (Paris: Belfond, 1971), with an introduction by Guérin, pp. 7–48; *Rosa Luxemburg et la spontanéité révolutionnaire* (Paris: Flammarion, 1971). Typically for Guérin, the second half of the latter volume brings together a number of texts representing different opinions on the subject. The following year he took part in a debate with Gilbert Badia, Michael Löwy, Madeleine Rebérioux, Denis Vidal-Naquet and others on the contemporary relevance of Luxemburg's ideas. Gilbert Badia et al., 'Rosa Luxemburg et nous: Débat', *Politique aujourd'hui: Recherches et pratiques socialistes dans le monde* (1972), pp. 77–106. Looking back at the revival of interest in Luxemburg in the 1960s and 70s, Löwy recently commented: 'There seems to be a hidden connection between the rediscovery of Rosa Luxemburg and eras of heightened contestation.' Löwy, 'Rosa Luxemburg, un Marxisme pour le XXIe siècle',

p. 59, *Contretemps* 8 (2010), pp. 59–63. This is a special issue devoted to Luxemburg's continuing relevance to revolutionary politics.

96. Guérin, 'Anarchisme et Marxisme', p. 233. As the co-editor (with Jean-Jacques Lebel) of a collection entitled 'Changer la Vie' for the publisher Pierre Belfond, Guérin took the opportunity to republish Trotsky's *Our Political Tasks* (1904), in which the young Trotsky was very critical of Lenin's 'Jacobinism' and of what he called the 'dictatorship over the proletariat': Léon Trotsky, *Nos tâches politiques* (Paris: Belfond, 1970). Luxemburg's 'Organizational Questions of Russian Social Democracy' is also included in the volume as an appendix. It is noteworthy that the English-language version of *Our Political Tasks*, produced in the 1970s by the Trotskyist New Park Publications, omits the sections in which Trotsky was most critical of Lenin. (Unfortunately, the Marxists Internet Archive have used the same partial translation.)

97. Guérin, 'Anarchisme et Marxisme', p. 252.

98. Guérin, À la recherche, pp. 10–1.

99. Guérin, 'Pourquoi communiste libertaire?', in À *la recherche*, p. 17.

100. Guérin, 'Un communisme libertaire, pour quoi?', À la recherche, pp. 123–5. Cf. Bookchin's remark that 'the problem is not to "abandon" Marxism, or to "annul" it, but to transcend it dialectically': Murray Bookchin, 'Listen, Marxist!' in *Post-Scarcity Anarchism* (Montréal: Black Rose Books, 1971), p. 177.

101. Nicolas Walter, 'Daniel Guerin's Anarchism', *Anarchy* vol. 8, no. 94 (1968), pp. 376–82. Guérin was not entirely unknown to English readers at the time. *Freedom* had published a translation of a 1966 interview on 30 September 1967.

102. George Woodcock, 'Chomsky's Anarchism' in *Freedom*, 16 November 1974, pp. 4–5.

103. Miguel Chueca, 'Anarchisme et Marxisme. La tentative de Daniel Guérin d'unir les deux philosophies et 'l'anarchisme' de Marx vu par Maximilien Rubel' in *Réfractions* no. 7, available at http://www.plusloin.org/refractions/refractions7/chueca1.htm (accessed 29 August 2006).

104. Ian Birchall, 'Daniel Guérin's Dialogue with Leninism' in *Revolutionary History* vol. 9, no. 2 (2006), pp. 194–5.

105. See Irène Pereira, *Un nouvel esprit contestataire. La grammaire pragmatiste du syndicalisme d'action directe libertaire* (Unpublished PhD, Ecole des Hautes Etudes en Sciences Sociales, Paris, 2009; supervised by Luc Boltanski); Patrice Spadoni, 'Daniel Guérin ou le projet d'une synthèse entre l'anarchisme et le Marxisme' in Philippe Corcuff and Michaël Löwy (eds.), *Changer le monde sans prendre le pouvoir? Nouveaux libertaires, nouveaux communistes*, special issue of *Contretemps*, no. 6 (February 2003), pp. 118–26; Olivier Besancenot and Michael Löwy, *Affinités révolutionnaires: Nos étoiles rouges et noires—Pour une solidarité entre marxistes et libertaires* (Paris: Editions Mille et Une Nuits, 2014). Guérin's daughter Anne has claimed recently that Guérin was the 'Maître à penser' of both Daniel Cohn-Bendit and the

Trotskyist Alain Krivine—Biographical preface to Daniel Guérin, *De l'Oncle Tom aux Panthères noires* (Pantin: Les Bons caractères, 2010), p. 8. See also Christophe Bourseiller's comment that "the politics of the *Mouvement communiste libertaire* derived largely from the theoretical reflexion of Daniel Guérin." *Histoire générale de "l'ultra-gauche"* (Paris: Editions Denoël, 2003), p. 484. In 1986 Guérin also contributed to the UTCL's 'Projet communiste libertaire', which was republished by Alternative Libertaire in 1993 and again in 2002: *Un projet de société communiste libertaire* (Paris: Alternative Libertaire, 2002). The 'Appel pour une alternative libertaire' of 1989 (which ultimately led to the creation of AL) was also co-written by Guérin: see Guérin, *Pour le communisme libertaire* (Paris: Spartacus, 2003), pp. 181–6.

106. Guérin, À la recherche, p. 10.

107. Guérin, 'Un communisme libertaire, pour quoi?', in À la recherche, p. 123.

DANIEL GUÉRIN

FOR A LIBERTARIAN COMMUNISM

■ WHY "LIBERTARIAN COMMUNIST"?

My education was anti-Stalinist Marxist. But for a good long while I have been foolhardy enough to draw heavily on the treasure chest of libertarian thought, ever relevant and alive on condition that it is first stripped of a not insignificant number of childish, utopian, and romantic notions as little useful as they are out of date.

Hence a misunderstanding that is all but inevitable but embittered by a certain bad faith on the part of my opponents: the Marxists have turned their backs on me as an anarchist, and the anarchists, because of my Marxism, have not always wanted to view me as one of them.

A young, neophyte—and hence sectarian—Marxist even thought he saw in my writings the assuaging of a consciousness that was "torn" between Marxism and anarchism and tossed desperately back and forth between the two, when in fact it is without the least such vacillation or any concern for my personal intellectual comfort that I believe in both the need for and the practicability of a synthesis between Marxism and anarchism.

Recently a working-class newspaper of Trotskyist bent and, let it be said in passing, of high quality, assured its readers that I had gone over from Marxism to anarchism. Taking advantage of the right to respond that was democratically afforded me, I responded to this inaccurate statement, the fruit of a basic need to catalogue everyone, that I was making "a contribution to the search for a synthesis between Marxism and anarchism." "A synthesis," I added, "that since May '68 has moved from the realm of ideas to that of action."

Note: The paragraphs in square brackets were present in the original 1969 version of this article ('Pourquoi "marxiste libertaire"?'), but omitted from subsequent editions.

But I was still seeking a denomination, since in order to communicate we all need a label. The one I had decided on ten years ago, that of "libertarian socialist," no longer seemed to me appropriate, for there are many kinds of socialism, from social democratic reformism to "revisionist communism" and an adulterated humanism. In short, the word "socialism" belongs to the category of debased words.

[Italian students with whom I had debated Marxism and anarchism in general and self-management in particular, provided me with the label: these young people call themselves libertarian Marxists. In truth this is not a discovery: the protesters of May in France, red and black flags mixed together, were libertarian Marxists, without being aware of it or calling themselves such.]

Hence the title of this book. Assembled here are a certain number of texts, varied in their subject matter and the periods in which they were written, but which all converge from various roads on the approach to a libertarian communism.

The short book published under the title *Anarchism* might have created a double misunderstanding: that I espoused all the ideas laid out in it for information purposes, and also that I showed myself unable to draw from this digest a synthesis of my own devising, which would be valid in the present and the future.[1] This supposition was doubly inexact, for I willingly effaced myself before the subject. In the present collection I attempt to fly with my own wings. At my own risk.

[The materials presented here are followed by the date they were written, though some retouching was done in order to bring the style and content up to date.]

The revolution that is rising before us will be—already is—libertarian communist.

[May 1969]

Notes

1.   Guérin is referring to *L'Anarchisme, de la doctrine à la pratique* first published in 1965 by Gallimard. It was published in English as *Anarchism: From Theory to Practice* (Monthly Review Press, 1970), with an Introduction by Noam Chomsky. [DB]

■ THE REHABILITATION OF ANARCHISM

Anarchism has long been a victim of an undeserved discredit, of an injustice that has manifested itself in three ways.

First, its defamers insist that anarchism is dead, that it has not resisted the great revolutionary tests of our time: the Russian Revolution and the Spanish Revolution. That it no longer has a place in the modern world, characterized as this is by centralization, large-scale political and economic units, and the totalitarian concept. All that is left to the anarchists, as Victor Serge said, is, "by the force of events to go over to revolutionary Marxism."[1]

Second, its detractors, in order to better discredit it, propose an absolutely tendentious vision of its doctrine. Anarchism is said to be essentially individualist, particularist, and resistant to any form of organization. It aims at fracturing and atomizing, at the retreat into themselves of local units of administration and production. It is said to be incapable of unity, centralization, and planning. It's nostalgic for "the Golden Age." It aims for the reviving of outmoded forms of society. It sins by a childish optimism; its "idealism" fails to take into account the solid reality of the material infrastructure.

Finally, certain commentators are interested solely in wresting from oblivion and publicizing only its most controversial deviations, like individual assassinations and propaganda by the deed.

In revisiting the question I'm not simply trying to retrospectively repair a triple injustice or trying to write a work of erudition. It seems to me, in fact, that anarchism's constructive ideas are still alive; that they can, on condition they be reexamined and closely scrutinized, assist contemporary socialist thought in making a new start.

Nineteenth-century anarchism is clearly distinguishable from twentieth-century anarchism. Nineteenth-century anarchism was essentially doctrinal. Though Proudhon had played a more or less central role in the revolution of 1848, and the disciples of Bakunin were not totally foreign to the Paris Commune, these two nineteenth-century revolutions in their essence were not libertarian revolutions, but to a certain extent rather "Jacobin" revolutions. On the contrary, the twentieth century is, for the anarchists, one of revolutionary practice. They played an active role in the two Russian Revolutions and, even more, in the Spanish Revolution.

The study of the authentic anarchist doctrine, as it was formed in the nineteenth century, shows that anarchy is neither disorganization, disorder, nor atomization, but the search for true organization, true unity, true order, and true centralization, which can only reside, not in authority, coercion, or compulsion exercised from the top down, but in free, spontaneous, federalist association from the bottom up. As for the study of the Russian and Spanish revolutions and the role played in them by the anarchists, it shows that contrary to the false legend believed by some, these great and tragic experiences show that libertarian socialism was largely in the right against the socialism I'll call "authoritarian." Throughout the world, socialist thought over the course of the fifty years that followed the Russian Revolution, of the thirty years that followed the Spanish Revolution, has remained obsessed with a caricature of Marxism, bursting with its dogmas. In particular, the internecine quarrel between Trotsky and Stalin, which is the one best known to the advanced reader, if it contributed to wresting Marxism-Leninism from a sterilizing conformism, did not truly cast complete light on the Russian Revolution, because it did not address—could not address—the heart of the problem.

For Voline, anarchist historian of the Russian Revolution, to speak of a "betrayal" of the revolution, as Trotsky does, is insufficient as an explanation: "How was that betrayal possible in the aftermath of so beautiful and total a revolutionary victory? This is the real question. . . . What Trotsky calls betrayal was, in fact, the ineluctable effect of a slow degeneration due to incorrect methods. . . . It was the degeneration of the revolution . . . that led to Stalin, and not Stalin who caused the revolution to degenerate." Voline asks: "Could Trotsky really 'explain' the drama since, along with Lenin, he himself contributed to the disarming of the masses."[2]

The assertion of the late, lamented Isaac Deutscher, according to which the Trotsky-Stalin controversy would "continue and reverberate for the rest of the century" is debatable.[3] The debate that should be reopened and continued is perhaps less that between Lenin's successors, which is already outdated, but rather that between authoritarian socialism and libertarian socialism. In recent time anarchism has come out of the shadow to which it was relegated by its enemies.

Materials for a fresh examination of anarchism are today available to those who are impassioned about social emancipation and in search of its most effective forms. And also, perhaps, the materials for a synthesis, one both possible and necessary, between the two equally fertile schools of thought: that of Marx and Engels and that of Proudhon and Bakunin. Ideas, it should be said, contemporary in their flowering and less distant from each other than might be thought. Errico Malatesta, the great Italian anarchist, observed that all the anarchist literature of the nineteenth century "was impregnated with Marxism."[4] And in the other direction, the ideas of Proudhon and Bakunin contributed in no small degree to enriching Marxism.

[1965]

Notes

1. Serge's preface to Joaquín Maurín, *Révolution et Contre-Révolution en Espagne* (Rieder, 1937).
2. See Voline's *The Unknown Revolution, 1917–1921* (Book 2, Part V, Ch. 7), first published in French in 1947. Voline was the pseudonym of Vsevolod Mikhailovich Eikhenbaum (1882–1945), a prominent Russian anarchist who took part in both the Russian and Ukrainian revolutions before being forced into exile by the Bolsheviks. [DB]
3. See Deutscher's biography of Trotsky, *The Prophet Armed, The Prophet Unarmed* and *The Prophet Outcast* (first published 1954–63).
4. Malatesta, polemic of 1897 quoted by Luigi Fabbri, *Dittoturae Rivoluzione* (1921).

■ PROUDHON AND WORKERS' SELF-MANAGEMENT

The problem is one with a certain topicality. In effect, it revolves around the question already touched on by the social reformers of the nineteenth century and posed with even more perplexity by the men of today: who should manage the economy? Is it private capitalism? Is it the state? Is it the associated workers? In other words, three options existed and continue to exist: free enterprise, nationalization, and socialization, i.e., self-management.

From 1848 Pierre-Joseph Proudhon was the ardent advocate of the third solution. In this he set himself apart from the socialists of his time, supporters of at least transitional state management. Their spokesman was Louis Blanc in his pamphlet on *The Organization of Labor* (1840).[1] It was Louis Blanc who was Proudhon's *bête noire*, rather than Marx and Engels, whose *Communist Manifesto*, written in German in 1847, he was not aware of. Louis Blanc's influence makes itself felt in the *Manifesto*, where it was a question of "centralizing all the instruments of production in the hands of the state." State centralization crops up constantly in it, like a litany: "Centralization of credit in the hands of the state with state capital and its exclusive monopoly." "Centralization in the hands of the state of all means of transport." "The organization of industrial armies, particularly for agriculture."

It's true that the authors of the *Manifesto*, still following Louis Blanc, envisaged a later stage, no longer statist but clearly libertarian, from which, the proletariat having destroyed classes and thus class antagonism, the state would disappear and production would—finally—be managed by the workers.

But the end of the transitional statist period was relegated to a distant future, was more or less considered utopian and, because of this, it was felt unnecessary to lay out the problems of workers' self-management before its time. When one reads Marx one is surprised at the rarity, the brevity, and the summary nature of the passages concerning the free association of producers. On the other hand Proudhon who, because he was of working-class origins and upbringing, considered self-management a concrete, immediate problem, studied its functioning in depth and in detail. This is why those of our contemporaries who consider the problem of self-management or who try to put it into practice gain far more from the works of Proudhon than from those of Marx. Before trying to lay out the Proudhonian conception of workers' self-management it is necessary to briefly recall, in contrast, his rejection of "authoritarian" management of the economy. Since he could not have read the *Communist Manifesto* and could only have had imperfect knowledge of Marxist thought, notably through the *Poverty of Philosophy*, written in French, it is principally against Louis Blanc, his compatriot and direct adversary, that Proudhon multiplied his attacks:

"The state is the patrimony, it's the blood and the life of Louis Blanc. Hit out at the state and Louis Blanc is a dead man."

"Once the economic revolution is accomplished, must the state and the government remain? With the economic revolution . . . the state should completely disappear."[2]

"The instruments of production and exchange should not be entrusted to the state. Being to the workers what the hive is to bees, their management should be entrusted to workers' associations."[3] Only thus "large-scale industry which, through the alienation of popular power, lowers the wage earner to a state worse than slavery, becomes one of the main organs of freedom and public happiness."[4] "We associated producers or those on the path of association," Proudhon proclaims in the style of a manifesto, "have no need of the state. . . . Exploitation by the state is still monarchy, still wage labor. . . .We no more want government of man by man than exploitation of man by man. Socialism is the opposite of governmentalism. . . . We want these associations to be . . . the first nucleus of a vast federation of companies and enterprises, united by the common bond of the democratic and social republic."[5]

Let us now see what the workers' self-management which Proudhon opposed to the transitional state management dear to both Louis Blanc and Karl Marx consisted of.

The revolution of February 1848 saw a spontaneous blossoming of workers' productive associations born in Paris and Lyon. It was this nascent self-management, rather than the political revolution, which was, for the Proudhon of 1848, "the revolutionary fact." It had not been invented by a theoretician or preached by doctrinaires. It was not given its initial impetus by the government. It came from the people. And Proudhon implored the workers throughout the republic to organize in the same way; that they draw to them, first small property, small merchants, and small industry, then large property and large enterprises, and then the most extensive operations (mines, canals, railroads, etc.), and in so doing "become the masters of everything."[6]

There's a tendency today to only recall Proudhon's desire, naive to be sure, and doubtless anti-economic, to ensure the survival of small-scale artisanal and commercial enterprise. There is certainly no lack of texts where Proudhon takes the side of small producers. Georges Gurvitch observed in the rich little book he dedicated to Proudhon that the writer had entitled a postscript to his *Confessions of a Revolutionary* (1851): "Apotheosis of the middle class," and that he'd "dreamed of a reconciliation of the proletariat and the middle class."[7] In his posthumous book, *The Theory of Property*, Proudhon made the following clarification:

"The object of workers' associations is not to replace individual action by collective action, as was madly believed in 1848, but rather that of ensuring all the entrepreneurs of small and middle industry the benefit of the discoveries, machines, improvements and procedures otherwise unavailable to modest enterprises and fortunes."[8]

But Proudhonian thought is ambivalent on this point. Proudhon was a living contradiction. He railed against property, the source of injustice and exploitation, and celebrated it to the extent that he saw in it a guarantee of personal independence. What is more, we too often have the tendency to confuse Proudhon with the tiny so-called Proudhonian coterie that, according to Bakunin, formed around him in the final years of his life. This fairly reactionary coterie was, he said, "stillborn."[9] Within the first International it vainly attempted to oppose private ownership of the means of production to collectivism. And if it did not live long it was mainly because most of its followers, easily convinced by

Bakunin's arguments, did not hesitate to abandon their supposedly Proudhonian concepts in favour of collectivism.

In any case, the last Mutualists, as they called themselves, only partially rejected collective property. They only fought against it in agriculture, given the individualism of the French farmer, but they accepted it in transport, and in the case of industrial self-management they called for the thing while rejecting the name.[10] If they were so afraid of the name it was mainly because the temporary united front formed against them by Bakunin's collectivist disciples and certain authoritarian Marxists, barely disguised supporters of state management of the economy—like Lucraft at the Basel Congress[11]—did nothing to reassure them. Marxist defamation did the rest, attributing to Proudhon the somewhat reactionary point of view of his epigones.

In fact, Proudhon was in step with his time. As Pierre Haubtmann pointed out in his magisterial thesis, "He has often been incorrectly presented as hostile to the very principle of large-scale industry. There is no doubt that at the sight of the Moloch factory—like the tentacular state—he reflexively recoils in fear, which leads him, in reaction, to lean towards small businesses and decentralization. But as concerns economic life, it would be a serious error to think that he was hostile to the principle of mass production. On the contrary, he speaks to us at length and enthusiastically of the need for powerful workers' productive associations. Of their role and their grandiose future. He thus accepts and even desires large-scale industry. . . . But he wants to humanize it, to exorcise its evil power, to socialize it by handing its fate over to a community of workers, equal, free, and responsible."[12] Proudhon understands it is impossible to go backwards. He is realistic enough to see, as he writes in his *Notebooks*, that "small-scale industry is as foolish as small-scale culture."[13]

As for large-scale modern industry, demanding a significant number of workers, he is decisively collectivist: "In the future large-scale industry and large-scale agriculture must be born of association."[14]

In *General Idea of Revolution in the Nineteenth Century* (1851) Proudhon several times returned to this modernist and, I might say, futurist concept: "The workers' companies, a protest against wage labor, are called on to play a considerable role in the near future. This role will above all consist in the management of the great instruments of labor and of certain tasks, which "demand' both a great division of functions and a great collective force."[15]

In his *Justice* (1858) Proudhon waxes indignant that people have dared to present him as an enemy of technical progress.[16] In his final work, which appeared shortly after his death, *On the Political Capacity of the Working Class*, he again confirms: "The construction of railroads should have been entrusted to workers' companies. If it's a matter of large-scale manufacturing, extractive, maritime or steel industries, it is clear that there is place for association. No one any longer contests this."[17]

In my book *Anarchism* I already listed the essential conditions for workers' self-management:

- Every associated individual has an undivided share in the property of the company.
- Every worker must assume his share of unpleasant and difficult tasks.
- He must pass through a variety of work and instruction and positions in the company that ensure him an encyclopedic education. Proudhon insists absolutely on "having the worker go through the series of industrial operations to which he is connected. In this way the division of labor can no longer be a cause of degradation for the worker; on the contrary, it is the instrument of his education and the guarantor of his security."[18]

Pierre Haubtmann, commenting on Proudhon, remarked that for Marx it's the "automatic workshop"—we would say automation—which, through the division of labor and the reduction of working hours, both pushed to the extreme, will allow every man to achieve "total development." Machinery extending man, disalienation will enter into play, not in work, but in leisure. Proudhon is hardly seduced by such a perspective. For him, man is essentially a producer. He wants him to constantly be at work. We're at antipodes from the exuberant *Right to be Lazy* by Paul Lafargue.[19] For the ferocious Puritan, for the "Saint Paul of socialism" that Proudhon was, leisure is not far from being a synonym for lust.[20] He expects "disalienation" from a mode of production that would give the worker a synthetic vision of the labor process.[21]

Gurvitch, contrasting Marx and Proudhon, underlines the following passage from *Justice*: "The spirit is no longer in the worker; it has passed over to the machine. What should be the virtue of the worker has become his degradation." This evil can only be corrected "if the collective forces alienated for the profit of a few exploiters are returned to labor as a whole."[22]

Proudhon counts on an increase in productivity under self-management, thanks to the joy of disalienated labor.

After this digression, according to Proudhon the essential conditions of self-management are:

- Functions are elective and the rules are submitted for the approval of the associates.
- Remuneration is proportional to the nature of the function, the importance of the talent, and the breadth of the responsibility. Each associate participates in the profits in proportion to his services.
- Everyone is free to quit the association at will, to regulate his hours, and liquidate his share.
- The associated workers select their leaders, their engineers, their architects, and their accountants. Proudhon insists on the fact that the proletariat is still lacking in certain abilities. It must be recognized that "due to the insufficiency of its insights and its lack of business expertise the working class is still incapable of managing interests as large as those involved in commerce and large-scale industry, and consequently falls short of achieving its destiny. Men are lacking among the proletariat."[23]

Hence the need to join to workers' self-management "industrial and commercial notables" who will initiate the workers in the disciplines of business and who will be paid a fixed wage: "There is room for everyone under the sun of the revolution."[24]

Let us note in passing that this libertarian understanding of self-management is at antipodes from the paternalistic and statist "self-management" laid out by Louis Blanc in a decree of September 15, 1849.[25] The author of *The Organization of Labor* wanted to create workers' associations under the aegis of and sponsored by the state. He envisioned an authoritarian division of profits: 25 percent for the amortization of capital, 25 percent for social assistance funds, 25 percent for reserve funds; 25 percent to be shared among the workers.

Proudhon wanted nothing to do with a "self-management" of this kind. No compromise was possible for an intransigent individual like him. The associated workers were not "to submit to the state," but "to be the state itself."[26] "The association . . . can do everything, reform everything without the assistance of the authorities, conquer and force authority itself to submit."

Proudhon wanted "to march to government through association and not to association through government."[27]

He warned against the illusion that the state, as dreamed of by the authoritarian socialists, could tolerate free self-management. How "could it accept, alongside a centralized power, the formation of enemy centers?" From which this warning, whose intransigence becomes prophetic: "Nothing is doable through the initiative, spontaneity, and independent actions of individuals and collectivities as long as they face the colossal force with which the state is invested by centralization."[28]

In fact, Proudhon anticipates here the tragedy of contemporary self-management, as experienced in both Yugoslavia and Algeria within the framework of a dictatorial state.

In fact, it is the libertarian and not the statist concept of self-management that prevailed at the congresses of the First International. At the Lausanne Congress (1867) the rapporteur, the Belgian César de Paepe, having proposed making the state the owner of the enterprises to be nationalized, Charles Longuet, at the time a libertarian, added: "Agreed, on the condition that it be understood that we define the state as the collective of citizens . . . and also that these services will not be administered by state functionaries but by workers' companies." The debate was picked up again the following year (1868) at the Brussels Congress and the same rapporteur was careful to make the requested rectification: "Collective property will belong to the entire society, but it will be conceded to workers' associations. The state will now be only the federation of various groups of workers." The proposal, thus, refined, was adopted.[29]

The optimism Proudhon demonstrated in 1848 relating to self-management was somewhat belied by the lesson of facts. A few years later, in 1857, he subjected the workers' organizations still in existence to a harsh critique. Their inspiration had been naive, illusory, and utopian. They had paid the price for inexperience. They had fallen into particularism and exclusivism. They had functioned like a collective managerial class and been swept along by the ideas of hierarchy and supremacy. All the abuses of capitalist societies "were exaggerated in these so-called fraternal companies." They had been torn by discord, rivalries, defections, and betrayals. Their managers, once they had been initiated into the business, had withdrawn "to set themselves up as bosses and bourgeois." Elsewhere, it was the associates who had called for the sharing out of products. Of the several hundred workers' associations created in 1848, twenty remained nine years later. And Proudhon opposed a notion of "universal" and "synthetic" self-management to that narrow and particularist mentality. The task for the future was far more than the "assembling into societies of a few hundred workers;" it was nothing less than "the economic reconstituting of a nation of thirty-six million souls." The future workers' associations, "instead of acting for the profit of a few," must work for all.[30] Self-management thus demanded "a certain education" of the self-managers. "One is not born an associate; one becomes one." The most difficult task of the associations was that of "civilizing the associates." What they had lacked—and here Proudhon renewed his warning of 1851—was "men issued from the working masses who had learned at the school of the exploiters to do without them." It was less a matter of forming "a mass of capital" than a "fund of men."[31]

On the legal plane Proudhon had initially envisaged entrusting the property of their enterprises to the workers' associations. Now, as Georges Gurvitch points out, he rejected his original notion "of ownership by groups of producers."[32] In order to do this he distinguished, in a posthumous work, between possession and property.[33] Property is absolutist, aristocratic, feudal, despotic; possession is democratic, republican, egalitarian: it consists in the usufructuary enjoyment of a non-cedable, indivisible and inalienable concession. The producers would receive, as "*allods*," like the ancient Germans, their instruments of production. They would not be the owners. This "higher formulation" of ownership would unite all the advantages of property and association without any of the drawbacks. What would succeed property would be, as Gurvitch says, federative co-property attributed not to the state, but to all the producers, united in a vast agricultural and industrial federation. The economic federation would come to "counterbalance" the state, a state this time not erased from the Proudhonian map, but transformed from top to bottom.

And Proudhon sees a revised and corrected self-management in the future: "It's no longer vain rhetoric that proclaims it: it's economic and social necessity. The moment approaches when we'll only be able to advance under these new conditions. . . . The classes . . . must be resolved into one sole association of producers."[34]

On what bases will the exchanges between the various workers' associations be ensured? Proudhon initially maintained that the exchange value of all merchandise could be measured by the amount of labor necessary for its production. The various production associations would sell their goods at cost. The workers, paid with "labor bonds," would purchase merchandise at exchange posts or in social stores at cost.

This so-called Mutualist conception was a tad utopian, in any case difficult to apply under capitalism. The People's Bank, founded by Proudhon in early 1849, succeeded in obtaining some 20,000 members in six weeks, but its existence was to be brief. To be sure, the sudden rise to power of Prince-President Louis Bonaparte had something to do with this. But it was illusory to think that Mutualism would spread and to exclaim as Proudhon did that "it was truly the new world, the society of "promise' which, grafted onto the old world, gradually transformed it!"

It appears that Pierre Haubtmann was correct in stressing in his thesis the illusory character of the Mutualism of the years 1846–1848. But he perhaps attacked Proudhon too vigorously in the way that he invokes the sins of his youth, which would quickly be corrected by his concrete and more positive visions of workers' self-management.

Remuneration based on the evaluation of working hours was debatable for various reasons. Around 1880 the anarchist communists (or "libertarian communists") of the school of Kropotkin, Malatesta, Elisée Reclus, Carlo Cafiero and others did not fail to criticize it. In the first place, in their eyes it was unjust: "Three hours of Peter's labor," Cafiero objected, "are often worth five hours of Paul's." Factors other than duration intervene in the determination of the value of labor: the intensity, the professional and intellectual education required, etc. We must also take into account the worker's family responsibilities. One finds the same objections in the *Critique of the Gotha Program*, written by Karl Marx in 1875, but hushed up by German social democracy until 1891, and which the libertarian communists thus were not aware of when they argued against Proudhon.

What is more, maintains the school of Kropotkin, under a collectivist regime the worker remains a wage earner, a slave to the community that purchases and keeps an eye on the quantity of his labor. Remuneration proportionate to the hours of labor furnished by each cannot be an ideal, but at best a temporary expedient. We must have done with morality based on accounting ledgers, with the philosophy of "must and have to."

This mode of remuneration proceeds from a watered down individualism in contradiction with collective ownership of the means of production. It is incapable of implementing a profound and revolutionary transformation of man. It's incompatible with anarchism. A new form of ownership demands a new form of remuneration: the services rendered society cannot be evaluated in monetary units. Needs must be placed above services. All the products produced by the labor of all should belong to all, and each should freely take his share. To each according to his needs; this must be the motto of libertarian communism.[35]

But Malatesta, Kropotkin, and their friends seem to have been unaware that Proudhon himself at least partially foresaw their objections and in the end revised his original conception. His *Theory of Property*, published posthumously, explained that it was only in his *First Memorandum on Property*, that of 1840, that he supported the equality of salaries to the equality of labor. "I had forgotten to say two things; first that labor is measured by a composite of duration and intensity; second, that there should not be included in the worker's wage either the amortization of his educational costs and the work he undertook on his own as a non-paid apprentice, or the insurance premiums against the risks he runs, and which are far from being the same in all professions."

Proudhon asserted he had "repaired" this "omission" in his subsequent writings, where he had the unequal costs and risks paid for by the mutual insurance cooperative societies.[36] We note here that Proudhon in no way considered the remuneration of association members a salary, but rather a distribution of profits, freely decided by associated workers and those jointly responsible. If not, as Pierre Haubtmann notes, self-management makes no sense.

The libertarian communists also reproached Proudhon's Mutualism and the more consistent collectivism of Bakunin for not having wanted to prejudge the form that the remuneration of labor would take under a socialist regime. These critics seem to lose sight of the fact that the two founders of anarchism were careful not to prematurely imprison society in a rigid framework. On this point they wanted to preserve the greatest latitude for the workers' associations. For Bakunin collectivism had to be practiced "under varied forms and conditions, which will be determined in each locale, in each region, and each commune by its degree of civilization and the will of the population."[37]

But the libertarian communists themselves provide the justification for this flexibility, for this refusal of premature solutions when, contrary to their impatient expectations, they insist that in the ideal regime of their choice "labor will produce much more than is needed for all." In fact, it is only when the era of abundance arrives that "bourgeois" norms of remuneration can give way to specifically "communist" norms. And not before this, as Marx and Lenin saw with a certain lucidity, though not without statist prejudice.[38]

In 1884, writing the program of an anarchist International still in a state of limbo, Malatesta admitted that communism would only be immediately realizable in extremely limited sectors and that "for the rest" one must "transitionally" accept collectivism. "In order to be realizable, communism requires a great moral development of the members of society, an elevated and profound feeling of solidarity that the revolutionary outburst will perhaps not suffice in producing, which is even more likely in that at the beginning the material conditions favoring such a development will be lacking."[39]

After Malatesta, the anarchist Fernand Pelloutier, having become a revolutionary syndicalist, would be even more categorical: "No one believes . . . that the imminent revolution will realize pure communism. Since it will in all likelihood break out before anarchist education has been completed, men will not be mature enough to absolutely rule themselves. We must take men as they are, as the old society left them to us."[40]

Among the norms inherited from bourgeois economics, there is one whose maintenance under collectivism or self-management raises thorny problems, to wit, competition. Just as in Proudhon's eyes private property in the products of labor constitutes a guarantee for the producer of their personal independence, competition is "the expression of social spontaneity," the guarantor of the "freedom" of associations. In addition, it constitutes, for a long time to come, an irreplaceable stimulant without which "an immense relaxation would succeed the ardent tension of industry." "Remove competition . . . and society, deprived of its motive force, would stop like a pendulum whose spring is loose."[41] Proudhon proposed practical recipes: "Vis-à-vis society, the workers' company commits to always providing the products and services requested of it at a price close to cost. . . . To this effect the workers' company forbids itself any [monopolistic] coalitions, accepts the law of competition, and places its books and archives at the disposal of society, which, as the sanction of its right of control, preserves the ability to dissolve it."[42] "Competition and association mutually support each other. . . . The most deplorable error of socialism is that of having regarded [competition] as the overturning of society. There can be no question of destroying competition. . . . It's a question of finding its equilibrium, I would even say its organization."[43]

This attachment to the principle of competition earned Proudhon the sarcasm of Louis Blanc. "We are unable to understand those who imagined some strange coupling of two opposing principles. Grafting association onto competition is a poor idea. It means replacing eunuchs with hermaphrodites."[44]

Louis Blanc wanted to "arrive at a uniform price" fixed by the state and to prevent any competition between the workshops of one industry. Proudhon replied that prices "are only settled by competition," that is, by the consumer's ability to "to do without the services of those who overstate them."[45]

To be sure, Proudhon did not hide the evils of competition, which he had abundantly described in his *Philosophy of Poverty*. He knew it was a source of inequality. He admitted that "in competition victory is assured to the largest battalions." As long as it is "anarchic" (in the pejorative sense of the term), as it only exists for the profit of private interests, it necessarily engenders civil war and, in the end, oligarchy. "Competition kills competition."[46]

But in Proudhon's opinion the absence of competition would be no less pernicious. He cited the example of the state-run tobacco office. This monopoly, from the very fact that it is free of competition, is too dear a service and its productivity is insufficient. If all industries were subject to such a regime, the nation, according to him, would no longer be able to balance its receipts and expenses.[47]

However the competition dreamed of by Proudhon is not the unfettered competition of the capitalist economy, but a competition endowed with a higher principle that "socializes" it; a competition that operates on the basis of an honest exchange in a spirit of solidarity; a competition which, while safeguarding individual initiative, will return the wealth currently diverted by capitalist appropriation to the collective.[48]

It is clear that there is something utopian in this conception. Competition and the so-called market economy inevitably produce inequality and exploitation, even if the departure point is a situation of perfect equality. They can only be joined to workers' self-management transitionally, as a necessary lesser evil while waiting for the development within the self-managers of a mentality of "sincerity of exchange," as Proudhon called it[49] and above all, when society has passed from the stage of penury to that of abundance and competition loses its entire raison d'être.

But in this transitional period it seems desirable that competition should be limited, as is the case today in Yugoslavia, to the sphere of the means of consumption, where it at least has the advantage of defending the interests of the consumer.[50]

Nevertheless, in Yugoslavia competition too often leads to excesses and irrationalities which the authoritarian adversaries of the market economy take pleasure in denouncing. Useful both as a stimulant to the spirit of enterprise and as a means of struggle against the high cost of living, it too often sustains among the

Yugoslavian self-managers a selfish and quasi-capitalist mentality from which concern for the general interest is absent.

It should be noted that workers' self-management in Yugoslavia is criticized by the Cubans and the Chinese, precisely because of its inability to reconcile competition and socialism.

Well before the authoritarian "communists" of today denounced the coupling of self-management and competition, the libertarian communists of the 1880s attacked the Proudhonian collectivist economy based on the principle of struggle, where all that would be done would be reestablishing among the competitors equality at the starting point in order to then cast them into a battle necessarily resulting in victors and vanquished, where the exchange of products would end by being carried out in accordance with supply and demand, "which would mean descending into competition, into the bourgeois world." This language very much resembles that of certain detractors of the Yugoslav experience in the communist world. They think it necessary to direct at self-management the hostility inspired in them by the competitive market economy, as if the two notions were inseparable from each other. This was—and I speak of him in the past tense—the case of Che Guevara, for example, who mistrusted self-management because he thought it synonymous with competition.[51]

Proudhon, to return to him, sees quite clearly that management by workers' associations can only be unitary. He insists on "the need for centralization and unity." I do not find in him "that provincialism closed to the wide world" that some think they saw. He asks the question: "Aren't the workers' companies for the exploitation of large-scale industries an expression of unity? What we put in place of government is industrial organization. What we put in place of political centralization is economic centralization."

For Proudhon, self-management is society finally "alive, organized;" "the highest degree of freedom and order which humanity can achieve." And in a burst of enthusiasm he exclaims, "Here we are free, emancipated from our embryonic shell. All relations have been inverted. Yesterday we walked upside down. We are changing our existence. This, in the nineteenth century, is the revolution."[52]

Nevertheless, despite his concern for unity, Proudhon dreads authoritarian planning, which is why he instinctively prefers to it competition of solidaristic inspiration. But, in a more consistent fashion, anarchism has since made itself the advocate for democratic and libertarian planning, elaborated from the bottom up by the confederation of self-managed enterprises.

It is in this way that Bakunin glimpsed the possibilities of a planning on a worldwide scale which open up to self-management: "The workers' cooperative associations are a new fact in history. We are witnessing their birth and we can only sense but not determine at this time the immense development that without any doubt will ensue and the new political and social conditions that will arise in the future. It is possible and even quite probable that one day, going beyond the limits of communes, provinces, and even current states, they will provide all of human society with a new constitution, divided not into nations, but into industrial groups." They will thus form "an immense economic federation" with, at its summit, a supreme assembly. In light of "data as broad as it is precise and detailed, of worldwide statistics, they will combine supply and demand in order to guide, determine, and distribute among the different countries the production of international industry in such a way that there will no longer be, or almost no longer be, commercial and industrial crises, forced stagnation, and any wasted effort or capital."[53]

The Proudhonian conception of management by workers' associations bore within it an ambiguity. It was not always specified if self-managed groups would remain in competition with capitalist enterprises, if, as is today said in Algeria, the socialist sector would co-exist with the private sector or if, on the contrary, production as a whole would be socialized and placed under self-management.

Bakunin, unlike his teacher Proudhon, whose ideas are hesitant on this point, is a consistent collectivist. He clearly sees the dangers of the coexistence of these two sectors. The workers, even associated, cannot assemble the capital capable of fighting against big bourgeois capital. And what is more, the danger exists that within the workers' association there will arise, from the contagion of the capitalist environment, "a new class of exploiters of the labor of the proletariat."

Self-management contains within it all the seeds of the economic emancipation of the working masses, but it can only develop all these seeds when "capital, industrial establishments, primary materials, and tools . . . will become the collective property of productive workers' associations, both industrial and agricultural, freely organized and federated among themselves." "The social transformation can only occur in a radical and definitive fashion by methods acting upon all of society," that is, by a social revolution transforming private property into collective property. In such a social organization the workers will collectively be their own capitalists, their own bosses. The only things left to private property will be "those things that are truly for personal use."[54]

As long as the social revolution has not been accomplished Bakunin, while admitting that productive cooperatives have the advantage of accustoming workers to managing their own affairs, that they create the first seeds of collective workers' action, thought that these islands within capitalist society could only have limited effectiveness, and he incited workers "to occupy themselves less with cooperation than with strikes."[55] As Gurvitch notes, this is the opposite position from Proudhon's, who nourished illusions about the rapid absorption of the capitalist economy by workers' self-management, underestimated the importance of unions and made too little of the right to strike.[56]

By Way of a Conclusion

Proudhon's ideas on self-management do not form a body of homogeneous doctrine, perfectly adjusted, free of any hesitation or ambiguity. Far from it. Contradictions abound in it.

There is a Mutualist Proudhon who defends, exalts, and attempts to save the independent small producer from the implacable wheel of progress and there is a resolutely collectivist Proudhon who does not hesitate to march with his time, with technical progress, with technology, with large-scale industry.

There is an optimistic Proudhon who in 1848 covers in flowers the spontaneously born workers' associations, and there is a pessimistic Proudhon who, a few years later, in 1857, will draw up a severe balance sheet of the failure of these associations.

There is a dreamer Proudhon who imagines Mutualism susceptible of partial application within the capitalist regime and who persuades himself that the socialist sector, from its own dynamism, will spread, and there is a Proudhon who is much more realistic, and as a result reticent on this point.

There is, as concerns the legal status of property under self-management, a disintegrationist Proudhon who, at first, envisages entrusting it to the workers' associations themselves in accordance with the principle "the factories to the workers," and there is an integrationist Proudhon who will later prefer placing all producers in one vast agricultural and industrial federation.

There is a simplistic Proudhon who proposes an extremely arguable definition of labor value, and there is a subtler Proudhon who then admits that the duration of labor cannot be the sole basis for this calculation and who strives to repair what he calls his "omissions."

There is the Proudhon who puts private property on trial, and there is a Proudhon who praises it, just as there is a Proudhon who celebrates the virtues of competition and there is a Proudhon who insists on its evils. It's only quite rarely that he succeeds in constructing a true synthesis of contradictory notions, and this is why he hides his failures while flattering himself only for having "balanced" the antinomies.

There is a decentralizing and federalist Proudhon, who mistrusts all planning for fear of reviving authority, and there is a Proudhon who does not hesitate to prescribe economic centralization and stresses the unitary character of production.

There is a Proudhon who, by affirming the capacities of the working class and its duty to radically separate itself from bourgeois institutions, opens the way to modern working-class syndicalism, and there is a Proudhon who underestimates struggles for specific demands, haunted as he is by the formation of workers' production cooperatives.

Here we touch on what is perhaps the most serious omission in the Proudhonian conception of self-management. It fails to be articulated and coordinated by an anarcho-syndicalism or a revolutionary syndicalism of the type that made possible the admirable experience of the Spanish collectivizations of 1936. When Proudhon alludes to "a vast agricultural and industrial federation," he fails to dig deeper in the syndicalist manner into that notion which, under his pen, remains unarticulated and vague.

There is a Proudhon who, in the first part of his militant life, was strictly concerned with economic organization, who mistrusted everything having to do with politics, and there is a second Proudhon who will cease neglecting the problem of territorial administration, who will base it on the autonomous commune,[57] though failing to connect in a sufficiently precise and coherent manner communal power on one side and workers' production associations on the other.

Finally, there is a Proudhon who categorically refuses any form of state—to the point that he issued a sectarian rejection of the sponsoring of workers' associations by a socialist-leaning state—and there is also a Proudhon who no longer considers himself an anarchist but rather a federalist, and who participates in the state.

These, briefly recalled, are some of the omissions and failings concerning workers' self-management in Proudhonian thought.

But alongside these weaknesses, how many lucid points of view, how many prophetic insights! The reader of Proudhon, if he is up to date on the concrete problems posed by the practice of self-management in Yugoslavia [in the 1950s and the early '60s], and in Algeria [from independence until Boumedienne's coup d'état, 1962–1965], constantly finds himself on familiar ground. Almost all the difficulties that form the drama of contemporary self-management can be found announced and described in Proudhon's writings. In it they are the object of heart-rending warnings, whether it's on the question of the incompatibility of the tentacular state and free self-management, or of the lack of men prepared for self-management, or of the lack of technical cadres, or of the unavoidability—at least during a transitional period—of a market economy containing a certain degree of competition, and, finally, on the difficulty of establishing total communism prematurely, which will only be practicable when abundance reigns and the consumer will only have to draw from the pile. On all these points Proudhon illuminates the future with a powerful spotlight.

But even when he hesitates, when he contradicts himself, when he changes his mind, he provides his reader with a precious lesson in relativism.

It is thrilling to witness the flowering of a creative mind ever in movement, forever seeking, never fixed, never dogmatic, tumultuous to be sure, sometimes allowing himself to be carried away by a quip, by improvisation, by failure to reflect, but capable of correcting himself, revising himself, of accepting lessons from the facts, of evolving in the light of experience.

And in any case Proudhon had his excuses. First, in laying the foundations for workers' self-management, he entered a domain so virgin and new that no one could serve as his guide. Second, the contradictions were less in his ideas than in the object they reflected. Workers' self-management, by its very nature, is contradictory. It is condemned to waver between two poles: on one side the autonomy of production groups, necessary so that each member feels truly free and "disalienated." On the other hand, the need for coordination in order to have the general interest prevail over selfish ones.

This coordination, I think, can be ensured under optimal conditions by revolutionary working-class syndicalism, which is best qualified to play such a role, since it is the direct and authentic emanation of the workers. But where it is lacking, where it is degenerated and bureaucratized, where it is insufficiently structured, where it is underestimated, tamed, regarded as a poor relation, like a fifth wheel, the role of coordinator inevitably falls to the state, a state which, by the force of circumstances, wants above all to perpetuate itself, to constantly extend its remit, to infringe on any forms of autonomy, to nibble away at freedom.

In the final analysis the most profound contradiction that rends workers' self-management springs from the historical backwardness of the education of the proletariat. The capitalist regime, as well as the unionism of immediate demands that is its corollary, did not prepare the workers, or prepared them poorly, for their self-management functions.

For an entire period they are thus obliged to seek outside their ranks the experts, technical cadres, accountants, etc. Where the cadres barely exist, as in Algeria, the functioning of self-management is seriously hindered: someone recently observed that Algerian self-management requires two hundred thousand accountants and the country's government envisages the accelerated education of twenty thousand. But where these experts exist, at least partially, their intrusion from without subordinates self-management.

"Guardianship organizations," when they provide technical assistance to self-managed enterprises, tend to substitute themselves for the self-managers and to become managers in their stead.

These serious drawbacks can only be eliminated when the fusion "of science and the working class" dreamed of by Ferdinand Lassalle and, after him, by Rosa Luxemburg will allow the abolition of guardianship. As the masses gradually educate themselves the social base upon which the guardians rest will fade away. They will only be "executive organs," controllable and revocable by the "conscious actions" of the workers.[58]

Socialism is fated to remain a vain word, a demagogic and hollow option, as long as the workers are not able to manage production for themselves, as long as they are enslaved, or allow themselves to be enslaved, by a parasitic bureaucracy imitating the bosses whose place they cannot wait to take.

In countries like Yugoslavia and Algeria, where self-management still suffers from many vices in its functioning, it at least has the advantage of allowing the masses to do their apprenticeship both in democracy and management, of stimulating their enthusiasm at work (on the condition, of course, of ensuring them—which is not always the case—equitable remuneration). It inculcates in them the sense of their responsibilities, instead of maintaining, as is the case under the yoke of the omnipotent state, millennial habits of passivity, submission, and the inferiority complex left to them by a slavish past.

At the end of such an apprenticeship self-management is, in a way, condemned to succeed. For if this is not the case socialism will have failed in its historical mission. As Proudhon observed: "Upon the response that will be given . . . depends the entire future of the workers. If that response is in the affirmative a new world opens before humanity. If it is in the negative, the proletariat can give up all hope . . . : In this world there is no hope for them."[59]

[1965, in *Pour un Marxisme libertaire*]

Notes

1. Louis Blanc (1811–1882) was a leading socialist reformer who popularised the demand, "From each according to their abilities, to each

according to their needs." A member of the republican provisional government installed after the revolution of February 1848, he would later be a member of parliament under the Third Republic, sitting with the extreme left. In 1848, he famously pushed for the creation of cooperative workshops, to be financed at least initially by the state, in order to provide employment and promote cooperativism within a framework of economic regulation. [DB]

2. *Idée générale de la Révolution au XiXème siècle* (1851; 1926 edition), pp. 363–4. [These quotes are from the first article in a polemic between Proudhon and Blanc entitled 'Resistance to the Revolution', extracts in *Property Is Theft! A Pierre-Joseph Proudhon Anthology* (Oakland: AK Press, 2011). —DB]

3. *Idée générale de la Révolution au XiXème siècle* (1851; 1926 edition), pp. 277–8, 329. ['General Idea of the Revolution in the Nineteenth Century', *Property Is Theft!*, pp. 583–4, 595 —DB]

4. *Idée générale de la Révolution au XiXème siècle* (1851; 1926 edition), pp. 280. [Ibid., *Property Is Theft!*, p. 585 —DB]

5. 'Election Manifesto', *Le Peuple*, 8 November 1848. ['Election Manifesto of Le Peuple', *Property Is Theft!*, pp. 376–8.]

6. Ibid., p. 375.

7. Georges Gurvitch, *Proudhon* (PUF, 1965).

8. *Théorie de la propriété* (A.Lacroix, Verboeckhoven & Cie, 1866), p. 183.

9. *Archives Bakounine* (Champ Libre, 1973–83), ed. Arthur Lehning, vol. I, p. 241.

10. James Guillaume, *Le Collectivisme de l'Internationale* (Neuchâtel, 1904), p. 12.

11. Benjamin Lucraft, 1809–1897, was a craftsman from London, a leading Chartist and a member of the committee of the International Working Men's Association. As a delegate to the Basel congress (1869), he argued not only for land nationalisation, but for the large-scale cultivation of the land by the state on behalf of the people. [DB]

12. Pierre Haubtmann, *P.J. Proudhon, genèse d'un antithéiste* (unpublished doctoral thesis), pp. 994–5. [Haubtmann also published several books on Proudhon's life and work. —DB]

13. *Carnets*, vol. III, p. 114.

14. Ibid. [See K. Steven Vincent, *Pierre-Joseph Proudhon and the Rise of French Republican Socialism* (New York/Oxford: Oxford University Press, 1984), p. 156 —DB]

15. *Idée générale de la Révolution au XiXème siècle* (1851; 1926 edition), p. 175 ; 'General Idea of the Revolution in the Nineteenth Century', *Property Is Theft!*, p. 558. [DB]

16. *De la Justice dans la Révolution et dans l'Eglise* (Marcel Rivière, 1858), vol. III, pp. 459–93, quoted in Georges Gurvitch, *Proudhon et Marx: une confrontation* (Centre de documentation universitaire, 1964), p. 93.

17. *De la capacité politique*, pp. 171 & 190. [Quotation from "The Political Capacity of the Working Classes," *Property Is Theft!*, p. 748; also see p. 759 —DB]

18. *Idée générale*, pp. 277–83 & 329. ["General Idea of the Revolution", *Property Is Theft!*, pp. 583–6 —DB]

19. Paul Lafargue, *Le Droit à la Paresse* (first published 1880).

20. See my study, 'Proudhon et l'amour unisexuel' in *Essai sur la révolution sexuelle après Reich et Kinsey* (Belfond, 1963).

21. See K. Marx, *Poverty of Philosophy* and Haubtmann, *P.J. Proudhon, genèse d'un antithéiste*, pp. 998–9.

22. *De la Justice*, vol. III, p. 91; Gurvitch, *Proudhon et Marx*.

23. *De la Justice*, vol. III, p. 115.

24. *Idée générale*, p. 283. [*General Idea of the Revolution* (London: Pluto Press, 1989), p. 224 —DB]

25. Proudhon, *Les Confessions d'un révolutionnaire pour servir à l'histoire de la révolution de Février (1848)* (Marcel Rivière, 1929 edition), pp. 257–60.

26. 'Manifeste de la démocratie anarchiste' [Manifesto of anarchist democracy] in *Le Peuple*, 22, 26 & 31 March 1848.

27. *Carnets*, vol. III, pp. 211 & 312.

28. *De la capacité politique* (Marcel Rivière, 1924 edition), pp. 329 & 403.

29. Jacques Freymond (ed.), *La Première Internationale* (Droz, 1962), vol. I, pp. 151 & 365–465.

30. 'Conclusion' in *Manuel du spéculateur à la Bourse* (Garnier, 1857).

31. Extracts from the conclusion of the *Stock Exchange Speculator's Manual* (1857) can be found in *Property Is Theft!*, pp. 610–7. [DB]

32. Gurvitch, *Proudhon et Marx*, pp. 46 & 108.

33. *Théorie de la propriété.*

34. Ibid.

35. Malatesta, *Programme et organisation de l'Association internationale des travailleurs* (Florence, 1884); Kropotkine, *La Conquête du pain* (Stock, 1890); Kropotkine, *L'Anarchie, sa philosophie, son idéal* (Stock, 1896), pp. 27–8 & 31; Kropotkine, *La Science moderne et l'Anarchie* (Stock, 1913), pp. 82–3 & 103. ["Program and Organisation of the International Working Men's Association", *The Method of Freedom: An Errico Malatesta Reader* (Oakland: AK Press, 2014); Kropotkin, *The Conquest of Bread* (Oakland: AK Press, 2006),

"Anarchy: Its Philosophy and Ideal" and "Modern Science and Anarchism" are contained in edited form in the Kropotkin anthology, *Anarchism: A Collection of Revolutionary Writings* (New York: Dover Press, 2002)].

36. *Théorie de la propriété*, p. 22.
37. Bakounine, *Œuvres* (Stock, 1895–1913), vol. VI, p. 401.
38. Marx, *Lettre sur le programme de Gotha*; Lénine, *L'Etat et la Révolution* (1917).
39. Malatesta, *Programme et organisation de l'Association internationale des travailleurs*. [*Method of Freedom*, pp. 47–8 —DB]
40. Fernand Pelloutier, 'L'anarchisme et les syndicats ouvriers', in *Les Temps nouveaux*, 2 November 1895. ['Anarchism and the Workers' Union' in *No Gods No Masters* (Oakland: AK Press, 2005), pp. 409–15 —DB]
41. *Philosophie de la misère*, in *Œuvres complètes* (A. Lacroix, Verboeckhoven & Cie, 1867), vol. I, p. 225.
42. *Idée générale de la Révolution au XiXème siècle*, p. 281. [*Property Is Theft!*, p. 585 —DB]
43. *Philosophie de la misère*, in *Œuvres complètes* (A. Lacroix, Verboeckhoven & Cie, 1867), vol. I, p. 208.
44. Ibid., p. 210.
45. Ibid.
46. Ibid., pp. 209, 211 & 234.
47. *Philosophie de la misère*, vol. I, pp. 186 & 215.
48. Ibid., pp. 209 & 217.
49. Ibid., vol. II, p. 414.
50. Albert Meister, *Socialisme et Autogestion, l'expérience yougoslave* (Seuil, 1964), p. 334.
51. Cf. Ernest Germain, 'La loi de la valeur, l'autogestion et les investissements dans l'économie des États ouvriers', in *Quatrième Internationale*, February–March 1964.
52. *Idée générale*, pp. 202–3, 301–2, 342, 420, 428.
53. 'Programme et statuts de la Fraternité révolutionnaire' (1865) in Max Nettlau, *Michel Bakounine* (London: 1896), vol. I, p. 224.
54. Bakounine, *Œuvres*, vol. V, pp. 216–8; *Archives Bakounine*, vol. 1, 2nd Part, article from *Al Rubicone*, 3 January 1872.
55. In *Archives*, vol. I, 2nd Part, p. 73.
56. Gurvitch, *Proudhon et Marx*, p. 113.
57. *De la justice*, vol. I, p. 320; *Contradictions politiques* (1862), p. 237 & 245–6.
58. Rosa Luxemburg, 'Masse et chefs' ['Geknickte Hoffnungen', 1903], in *Marxisme contre dictature* (Spartacus, 1974), pp. 36–7.
59. Proudhon, *Manuel du spéculateur*, 'Conclusion'.

■ THREE PROBLEMS OF THE REVOLUTION

Voline, libertarian historian of the Russian Revolution after having been an actor and witness, wrote, "A fundamental problem was left to us by the preceding revolutions: above all I mean those of 1789 and 1917. Arising in large part against oppression, animated by a powerful surge of freedom, and proclaiming freedom as their essential goal, why did these revolutions descend into new dictatorships carried out by other dominating and privileged strata, into a new slavery of the popular masses? What would the conditions be that would allow a revolution to avoid this sad end? Is this end due to passing factors, to errors or mistakes that could be avoided in the future? And in the latter case, what would be the means to eliminate the danger that threatens the imminent revolutions?"[1]

With Voline, I think that the two great historical experiences of the French and Russian Revolutions are indissolubly connected. Despite the differences in periods, environment, and "class content," the problems they raise, the pitfalls they ran up against, were fundamentally the same. At the very most, in the first revolution they manifested themselves in a more embryonic form than in the later one. And so the men of today can only hope to find the path to their future definitive emancipation if they are able to distinguish between what was progress and what was failure in these two experiences in order to draw the lessons for the future.

In my opinion the basic cause for the relative failure of the two greatest revolutions in history resides not, to borrow again from Voline, in "historic inevitability," or simply in the subjective "errors" of revolutionary actors. The revolution bears within itself a serious contradiction (a contradiction which fortunately—and we will return to the subject—is not irremediable and is attenuated with time): it can only arise, it can only vanquish if it issues from

the depths of the popular masses, from their irresistible spontaneous uprising; but although the class instinct drives the popular
masses to break their chains, they are yet lacking in education and
consciousness. And since, in their formidable but tumultuous and
blind drive towards liberty, they run up against privileged, conscious, educated, organized, and tested social classes, they can only
vanquish the resistance they meet if they succeed in obtaining in
the heat of the struggle, the consciousness, the science, the organization, and the experience they lack. But the very fact of forging the
weapons I have just listed summarily, and which alone can ensure
their superiority over the enemy, bears an immense peril within it:
that of killing the spontaneity that is the very spirit of the revolution; that of compromising freedom through organization; that of
allowing the movement to be confiscated by an elite minority of
more educated, more conscious, more experienced militants who,
to begin with, offer themselves as guides in order, in the end, to
impose themselves as chiefs and to subject the masses to new forms
of the oppression of man by man.

For as long as socialism has been capable of reflecting on this
problem, for as long as it has been aware of this contradiction, more
or less since the beginning of the nineteenth century, socialism has
not ceased to struggle with it, to waver between the two opposing
poles of freedom and order. Every one of its thinkers and actors has
laboriously and stumblingly striven, at the price of many hesita-
tions and contradictions, to resolve the fundamental dilemma of the
revolution. Proudhon, in his famous *Mémoire sur la Propriété* (1840),
thought he had found the synthesis when he optimistically wrote:
"the highest perfection of society is found in the unity of order and
anarchy." But a quarter of a century later he melancholically noted:
"These two ideas, freedom . . . and order, stand together. . . . They
cannot be separated, nor can one be absorbed in the other; we
must resign ourselves to living with both, with keeping them in
balance. . . . No political force has yet provided the true solution to
the harmony of freedom and order."[2]

Today an immense empire, constructed under the sign of
"socialism" (and of "communism"), seeks painfully, without design,
and sometimes convulsively to escape the iron shackles of an "order"
founded on coercion in order to find the road to freedom which its

millions of subjects, daily more experienced and conscious, aspire to. The problem has been posed in an ever-more-burning fashion, and the final word has not been spoken.

If we look at it more closely, the problem has three relatively distinct aspects, though they are intimately connected.

1. In the period of revolutionary struggle, what parts should spontaneity and consciousness, the masses and the leaders, play?
2. Once the old oppressive regime has been overthrown, what form of political and administrative organization must be substituted for the one just defeated?
3. Finally, who should administer the economy and how should it be administered after the abolition of private property (a problem that is posed in all its magnitude for the proletarian revolution but which was posed only embryonically for the French Revolution)?

On each of these three questions, the socialists of the nineteenth century hesitated, shilly-shallied, contradicted themselves, and confronted each other. Which socialists?

Broadly speaking, three main currents can be distinguished:

a. Those I will call authoritarian, the statists and centralists, some the heirs of the Jacobin and Blanquist tradition of the French Revolution, others of the German (or more precisely, Prussian) tradition of the military discipline of the State with a capital "S."[3]
b. Those I will call anti-authoritarian, the libertarians, some of them heirs of the direct democracy of 1793, of the communalist and federalist idea, and others of Saint-Simonian apoliticism aspiring to substitute "the administration of things" for political government.
c. Finally, the so-called scientific socialists (Marx and Engels), laboriously striving, not always coherently or successfully, and often for purely tactical reasons (for they had to make concessions to the two wings of the working-class movement) to reconcile the two aforementioned currents, to find

a compromise between the authoritarian and libertarian ideas.

Let us try to briefly summarize the attempts made by these three currents of socialist thought to resolve the three fundamental problems of the revolution.

Spontaneity and Consciousness

The authoritarians do not have faith in the capacity of the masses to achieve consciousness on their own and, even when they claim the contrary, they have a panic fear of the masses. If they are to be believed, the masses are still degraded by centuries of oppression. They need to be guided and led. A small elite of leaders must be substituted for them to teach them revolutionary strategy and lead them to victory.

The libertarians, on the contrary, maintain that the revolution must be the work of the masses themselves, of their spontaneity, of their free initiative, of their creative faculties, as unsuspected as they are formidable. They put people on guard against the chiefs who, in the name of greater consciousness, aspire to impose themselves on the masses in order to then despoil them of the fruits of their victory.

As for Marx and Engels, they at times placed the accent on spontaneity and at others on consciousness. But their synthesis remains a shaky, uncertain, and contradictory one. It must also be said that the libertarians do not always escape the same reproach. We find in Proudhon, juxtaposed to the optimistic exaltation of "the political capacity of the working classes," pessimistic passages in which he casts doubt on said capacity and joins the authoritarians in their suggestion that the masses must be led from above.[4] In the same way Mikhail Bakunin does not always succeed in ridding himself of the "48er" conspiratorialism of his youth and, immediately after relying on the irresistible primal instincts of the masses, he turns around and calls for the invisible "infiltration" of the latter by conscious leaders organized in secret societies. From which this strange back and forth: those he accuses, at times not without basis, of authoritarianism, catch him in the act of authoritarian Machiavellianism.

The two antagonistic tendencies of the First International mutually condemned each other, each with a certain amount of reason, for backstage maneuvers to ensure control of the movement.[5] We had to wait for Rosa Luxemburg for a more or less viable synthesis to be proposed between spontaneity and consciousness. But Trotsky compromised this laboriously obtained equilibrium in order to take the contradiction to its extreme. At certain moments he is "Luxemburgist." As can be seen in his *1905* (1907) and his *History of the Russian Revolution* (1930), he has a feeling and an instinct for revolution from below; he places the accent on the autonomous actions of the masses, but in the end, after having brilliantly combatted them, he rallies to Lenin's Blanquist conception of organization[6] and, once in power, he would act in a more authoritarian fashion than the leader of the school. Finally, in the harsh combat of his exile, he would shelter behind a now sanctified Lenin in order to put Stalin on trial, and this identification would prevent him until his final day from setting free the element of Luxemburgism within him.

The Question of Power

The authoritarians maintain that the popular masses, led by their chiefs, must substitute for the bourgeois state their own state adorned with the epithet "proletarian," and that, in order to ensure the permanence of the latter, they must push to the extreme the means of coercion used by the former (centralization, discipline, hierarchy, police). This schema draws from libertarians—and this for more than a century—cries of fright and horror. What is the use, they ask, of a revolution that would be satisfied with replacing one repressive apparatus for another? Uncompromising enemies of the state, of every form of state, they expect from the proletarian revolution the complete and definitive abolition of state coercion. They want to substitute the free federation of associated communes and bottom-up direct democracy for the old oppressive state.

Marx and Engels sought their way between the extremes of these two tendencies. They bore the Jacobin imprint, but on one hand contact with Proudhon around 1844 and the influence of Moses Hess,[7] and on the other the critique of Hegelianism and the discovery of "alienation" rendered them somewhat libertarian. They rejected the authoritarian statism of the Frenchman Louis Blanc as well as that of the German Lassalle.[8] They declared themselves supporters of the abrogation of the state. But only in the long run. The state, "the governmental hodgepodge," must continue in the aftermath of the revolution, but only for a time. As soon as the material conditions are realized that will allow for it to be done away with it will "wither away." And while waiting for that day, we must strive to "immediately attenuate as much as possible its most harmful effects."[9] This immediate perspective justly worries the libertarians. The survival, even "provisional," of the state says nothing good to them, and they prophetically announce that once reestablished the Leviathan will obstinately refuse to resign.[10] The libertarians' dogged criticism placed Marx and Engels in an embarrassing position, and there were times when they made so many concessions to their ideological adversaries that at a certain moment the debate over the state between socialists seemed to have no point or to be nothing but a simple quibble over words. Alas, this beautiful harmony lasted but a morning.

But the Bolshevism of the twentieth century reveals that this was not a simply verbal dispute. Marx and Engels' transitory state becomes, already in its embryonic form with Lenin and even more with Lenin's successors, a tentacular monster, which in no uncertain terms proclaims its refusal to wither away.

The Management of the Economy

Finally, what form of property should replace private capitalism?

The authoritarians have no hesitation in responding. Since their main defect is a lack of imagination, and since they fear the unknown, they fall back on forms of administration and management plagiarized from the past. The state will swoop up in its immense net all of production, all of exchange, all of finance. "State capitalism" will survive the social revolution. The bureaucracy, already gigantic under Napoleon, under the King of Prussia, and under the Tsar, will no longer be satisfied under a socialist regime with levying taxes and raising armies and increasing the police force: it will extend its tentacles over the factories, the mines, the banks, and the means of transport. The libertarians issue a cry of fright. This exorbitant expansion of the powers of the state looks to them to be the grave of liberty. Max Stirner was one of the first to rise up against the statism of the communist society.[11] Proudhon shouted no less loudly, and Bakunin followed him: "I detest communism," he declared in a speech, "because it necessarily arrives at the centralization of property in the hands of the state, while I . . . want the organization of society and collective and social property from the bottom up by way of free association, and not from the top down by means of some form of authority."[12]

But the anti-authoritarians are not unanimous in formulating their counter-proposal. Stirner suggests a "free association" of "egoists," too philosophical in inspiration and also too unstable. Proudhon, more concretely, suggests a combination—which in some ways is retrograde, petit-bourgeois, corresponding to the already outmoded state of small-scale industry—of small-scale commerce, of artisanal production: private property must be safeguarded. Small producers, remaining independent, must offer each other mutual aid. At the very most he accepts collective property in a certain number of sectors, which he agrees have already been conquered by large-scale industry: transport, mines, etc. But both Stirner and Proudhon, each in his own fashion, leave themselves open to the blistering critique administered them—a little unjustly, it must be said—by Marxism.

Bakunin for his part separates himself deliberately from Proudhon. For a brief time, he constituted a united front with Marx within the First International against his former teacher. He rejects post-Proudhonian individualism. He learns the lessons of industrialization. He calls for collective property. He presents himself as neither a communist nor a Mutualist but a collectivist. Production should be managed, both on a local basis by "the solidarization of communes" and on an occupational basis by groups or associations of workers. Under the influence of the Bakuninists the Basel Congress of the First International in 1869 decided that in the future society "the government will be replaced by councils of workers' organisations."[13] Marx and Engels waver and hedge. In the *Communist Manifesto* of 1848, inspired by Louis Blanc, they'd adopted the easy omni-statist solution. But later, under the influence of the Paris Commune of 1871 and the pressure of the anarchists, they would temper this statism and speak of "the self-government of the producers."[14] But these hints at anarchism would not last long and Marx and Engels would almost immediately return, in their fight to the death with Bakunin and his disciples, to a more authoritarian and statist phraseology.

So it is not totally without reason (though not always with total good faith) that Bakunin accused the Marxists of concentrating all of industrial and agricultural production in the hands of the state. In Lenin the statist and authoritarian tendencies, superimposed on an anarchism they contradict and annihilate, already exist in germ, and under Stalin, "quantity" being transformed into "quality," they degenerate into an oppressive state capitalism that Bakunin, in his occasionally unfair criticism of Marx, seems to have anticipated.

This brief historical reminder is only of interest insofar as it can assist us in orienting ourselves in the present. The lessons we will draw from them allow us to understand, in a striking and dramatic way, that despite many conceptions that seem today to be outmoded, childish, or proved wrong by experience (for example their "apoliticism"), on the essential questions the libertarians were in the right against the authoritarians. The latter let loose rivers of insults on the former, calling their program "a jumble of ideas from beyond the grave," reactionary utopias, outdated and decadent.[15] But it can be seen today, as Voline stresses, that it is the authoritarian idea that, far from belonging to the future, is nothing but a survival from the old, bourgeois world, worn out and moribund.[16] If there is a utopia, it is that of so-called state communism, whose bankruptcy is so patent that its own beneficiaries (concerned above all with safeguarding their interests as a privileged caste) seek today, laboriously and stumblingly, the means to amend it and evade it.

The future belongs neither to classical capitalism nor, as the late Merleau-Ponty tried to persuade us, to a capitalism revised and corrected by a "neoliberalism" or by social democratic reformism.[17] Their dual bankruptcy is no less resounding than that of state communism. The future still belongs, more than ever belongs, to communism, but a libertarian communism. As Kropotkin prophetically announced in 1896, our era "will bear the effects of the reawakening of libertarian ideas. . . . The next revolution will no longer be the Jacobin revolution."[18]

The three fundamental problems of the Revolution that we outlined above can and must finally find their solution. We are no longer in the era of the stammering, stumbling socialist thinkers of the nineteenth century. The problems are no longer posed abstractly, but rather concretely. Today we have at our disposal an abundant harvest of practical experiences. The technique of Revolution has been immensely enriched. The libertarian idea is no longer inscribed in the clouds, but emerges from the facts themselves, from the most profound and authentic aspirations, even when they are repressed, of the popular masses.

The problem of spontaneity and consciousness is easier to resolve today than a century ago. If the masses, as a result of the oppression they suffer, are still a bit behindhand in understanding the bankruptcy of the capitalist system, if they are still lacking in education and political lucidity, they have made up a large part of the historic delay. Everywhere, in the advanced capitalist countries, as well as in the developing countries and those subject to so-called communism, they have made a great leap forward. They are much harder to dupe. They know the full extent of their rights. Their knowledge of the world and their own destiny has been considerably enriched. If the deficiencies of the French proletariat prior to 1840, because of its inexperience and small numbers, gave birth to Blanquism, if that of the Russian proletariat before 1917 gave birth to Leninism, and that of the new, exhausted proletariat broken up following the civil war of 1918–1920 and those newly uprooted from the countryside gave birth to Stalinism, today the laboring masses have less need to abdicate their power into the hands of authoritarian and supposedly infallible tutors.

What is more, thanks notably to Rosa Luxemburg, the idea has penetrated socialist thought that even if the masses are not yet completely mature, even if the fusion of science and the working class dreamed of by Lassalle has not yet taken place, the only way to catch up and to remedy this deficiency is to assist the masses in doing their apprenticeship in direct democracy from the bottom up.[19] It is in developing, encouraging, and stimulating their free initiatives; it is in inculcating in them the sense of their responsibilities instead of maintaining in them, as state "communism" does (whether in power or in opposition), the age-old habits of passivity, submission, and feeling of inferiority passed on to them by a past of oppression. Even if this apprenticeship is at times difficult, even if the rhythm is at times slow, even if it cripples society with supplementary costs, even if it can only be effected at the cost of some "disorder," these difficulties, these delays, these supplementary costs, these growing pains, are infinitely less harmful than the false order, the false brilliance, the false "efficiency" of state "communism," which obliterate man, kill popular initiative, and finally dishonor the very idea of communism.[20]

As concerns the problem of the state, the lessons of the Russian Revolution are clearly written on the wall. Liquidating the power of the masses, as was done in the immediate aftermath of the triumph of the Revolution; reconstructing over the ruins of the former state machine a new oppressive apparatus even more perfected than the previous one, one fraudulently baptized "party of the proletariat," often by absorbing into the new regime the "experts" of the defunct regime (still imbued with their former authority); allowing the construction of a new privileged class which considers its own survival as an end in itself and which perpetuates the state that ensures that survival, is not the model to be followed. What is more, if we take literally the Marxist theory of the "withering away" of the state, the material conditions that had provoked and, according to the Marxists, legitimized the reconstruction of a state apparatus, should allow us today to do without that cumbersome gendarme so eager to remain in place that is the state.

Industrialization, though developing unevenly in each country, is taking giant steps throughout the world. The discovery of new sources of energy with unlimited possibilities is enormously accelerating this evolution. The totalitarian state engendered by poverty and which justifies itself by this poverty, daily becomes ever more superfluous. As for the management of the economy, all the experiments carried out, both in the quintessential capitalist countries like the United States as well as those in the countries subjected to state "communism," demonstrate that the future, at least for large sectors of the economy, no longer belongs to gigantic production units. Gigantism, which dazzled the late Yankee captains of industry as well as the communist Lenin, belongs to the past. *Too Big*: this is the name of a book on the evils of this plague on the American economy.[21] For his part Khrushchev, that wily boor, finally grasped, though late and timidly, the need for industrial decentralization. It was long believed that the sacrosanct imperatives of the planned economy demanded state management of the economy. Today it is realized that top-down planning, bureaucratic planning, is a frightful source of disorder and waste and, as Merleau-Ponty said, "It does not plan."[22] Charles Bettelheim showed us, in a book that was too often conformist at the time it was written, that it could only function efficiently if it was managed from the bottom up and not from the top down, if it emanated from the lower echelons of production and was constantly subject to their control—while in the USSR this control by the masses shines by its absence. Without any doubt, the future belongs to the autonomous management of enterprises by associations of workers. What remains to be worked out is the mechanism, delicate to be sure, of their federation, of the harmonizing of varied interests in a free order. From this point of view the attempt at a synthesis between anarchism and statism promoted by the now undeservedly forgotten Belgian socialist César de Paepe deserves exhumation.[23]

On other levels the evolution of technology and the organization of labor open the road to a socialism from the bottom up. The most recent research in the field of the psychology of work leads to the conclusion that production is only "efficient" if it does not crush man, if it associates instead of alienating him, if it appeals to his initiative, his full cooperation, and if it transmutes his drudgery into joyful labor, a condition that is not fully realizable either in the industrial barracks of private capitalism or those of state capitalism. What is more, the acceleration of the means of transport facilitates enormously the exercise of direct democracy. For example: thanks to airplanes, in a few hours the delegates of local branches of American labor unions—the most modern of which, such as those of the automobile workers, are dispersed across a whole continent—can be easily assembled.

But if we want to regenerate socialism, turned upside down by the authoritarians, and put it back on its feet, we must act quickly. In 1896 Kropotkin forcefully said that as long as socialism has an authoritarian and statist face it will inspire a certain mistrust in the workers and, because of this, it will see its efforts compromised and its later development paralyzed.[24] Private capitalism, historically condemned, only survives today because of the arms race on the one hand and the bankruptcy of state "communism" on the other. We cannot ideologically defeat big business and its so-called free enterprise, under cover of which a handful of monopolies dominate, we cannot see off nationalism and fascism, ever ready to rise from the ashes, unless we are capable of producing in practice a concrete substitute for state pseudo-communism. As for the so-called socialist countries, they will only escape their current impasse if we assist them, not in liquidating, but in completely rebuilding their socialism. Khrushchev came crashing down for having hesitated too long between the past and the future. The Gomułkas, Titos, and Dubčeks—despite their good will, their desire for de-Stalinization, and their antistatist tendencies—risk grinding to a halt, wobbling on the tightrope where they stand in an unstable equilibrium and, in the long run, will fail if they do not acquire the audacity and clear-sightedness that will allow them to define the essential bases for a libertarian communism.[25]

The Revolution of our time will be made from the bottom up— or it will not be made at all.

[1958, in *Jeunesse du Socialisme Libertaire*]

Notes

1. *La Révolution Inconnue, 1917–1921* (1969 edn.), p. 19. In *The Ego and Its Own* (1845), Max Stirner had already announced as the "principle of Revolution" this pessimistic axiom: "Always there is only a new master set in the old one's place, and the overturning is a—building up. . . . Since the master rises again as state, the servant appears again as subject." [English translation by Steven T. Byington (1907) —DB].

2. In *De la capacité politique des classes ouvrières* (Marcel Rivière edn., 1924), p. 200.

3. Louis-Auguste Blanqui (1805–1881), although from a bourgeois background, was a hugely influential revolutionary socialist republican and was involved in various attempted insurrections from an early age. 'Blanquism' is characterised by a lack of faith in working-class movements and by the belief that bourgeois society could only be destroyed by a violent coup effected by a small group of revolutionaries who would then introduce a new and more just social order. [DB]

4. Proudhon in *De la capacité*, pp. 88 & 119.

5. Cf. Karl Marx, *L'alliance de la démocratie socialiste et l'association internationale des travailleurs. Rapport et documents publiés par ordre du congrès international de La Haye* (London: A. Darson; Hamburg: O. Meissner, 1873).

6. See his *Terrorism and Communism* (1920).

7. An early socialist who met Marx and Engels in the 1840s, Hess (1812–1875) envisaged the realisation of the ideals of freedom and equality through the achievement of communism. [DB]

8. A contradictory figure in early German socialism, Ferdinand Lassalle (1825–1864) was a republican and democrat, and insisted on the necessary role of the state in socialism. [DB]

9. In Engels' 1891 preface to the first French edition of Marx, *La Guerre civile en France* (Bibliothèque d'études socialistes, 1901).

10. Thomas Hobbes' *Leviathan* (1651) is, among other things, an apologia for despotism.

11. See *The Ego and Its Own*.

12. Speech to the 1868 Bern congress of the Ligue de la paix et de la liberté, in *Mémoire de la Fédération jurassienne* (Sonvillier, 1873), p. 28.

13. Oscar Testut, *L'Internationale* (1871), p. 154.

14. Marx in *The Civil War in France*.

15. See the end of ch. 6 in Plekhanov, *Anarchisme et Socialisme, force et violence* (Librairie de l'Humanité, 1923), as well as the preface by Eleanor Marx-Aveling.

16. Voline, op. cit., pp. 218 and 229.

17. The philosopher Maurice Merleau-Ponty (1908–1961) was a prominent member of the left intelligentsia in the postwar years. Influenced by Marx, he was a member of the editorial committee of Sartre's review *Les Temps modernes* (until the two fell out in 1952); he also played a leading role in the *Union des Forces Démocratiques* created in 1958 by various elements of the non-communist left to oppose General Charles de Gaulle's attempt to become president of a reformed Republic. [DB]

18. Kropotkin, *L'Anarchie, sa philosophie, son idéal* (Stock, 1896), p. 51.

19. Cf. the 1904 text by Rosa Luxemburg reproduced as an appendix to the French translation of Trotsky, *Nos tâches politiques* (Belfond, 1970 [1904]). [This is a reference to Luxemburg's 'Organizational Questions of the Russian Social Democracy', available on the Marxists Internet Archive at https://www.Marxists.org/archive/luxemburg/1904/questions-rsd/index. htm; Guérin, with the anarchist artist Jean-Jacques Lebel, was the editor of the series in which Trotsky's *Our Political Tasks*, a critique of Lenin and Leninism, was published. —DB]

20. "Socialism" in the 1969 version published in D. Guérin, *Pour un Marxisme libertaire* (Laffont, 1969). [MA & DB]

21. Morris Ernst, *Too Big* (New York, 1940).

22. 'Réforme ou maladie sénile du communisme', *L'Express*, 23 November 1956.

23. César de Paepe, 'De l'organisation des services publics dans la société future', 1874, in *Ni dieu ni maître, anthologie de l'anarchisme*, 1969 edition, p.

317. [Now available in a slightly abridged translation in *No Gods No Masters: An Anthology of Anarchism* (Oakland: AK Press, 2005) —DB] Cf. G.D.H. Cole, *A History of Socialist Thought* (London: Macmillan, 1958), vol. II, pp. 204–7.

24. Kropotkin, op. cit., pp. 31–3.

25. The so-called Gomułka's thaw was a short period in 1956 when, encouraged by Khrushchev's famous speech to the Twentieth Congress of the Soviet Communist Party denouncing Stalin, the Polish Communist leader initiated a certain liberalization under the banner of a "Polish road to socialism." Tito's split with Stalin in 1948 and the adoption of the principle of self-management as the basis of a democratic socialist economy in 1950 meant that Yugoslavia was seen by many anti-Stalinist socialists in the west as a beacon of hope (which is why Yugoslavian self-management was discussed, albeit critically, in Guérin's 1965 book, *Anarchism: From Theory to Practice*). Alexander Dubček was the figurehead of the "Prague Spring" of 1968 whose aim was "socialism with a human face." All these attempts were crushed. [DB]

■ THE FRENCH REVOLUTION DE-JACOBINIZED

Today, we are surrounded by nothing but ruins. The ideologies that were drummed into us, the political regimes that we were made to submit to or were held up as models are all falling to pieces. As Edgar Quinet said, we have lost all our baggage.[1]

Fascism, the ultimate and barbarous form of man's domination of man, collapsed a quarter century ago in a bloodbath. And the very people who clung to it like a life raft, who had called it to the rescue against the working class, even at the point of foreign bayonets, got skinned in the adventure and are forced, even though they still secretly prefer it, to offer their merchandise in a camouflaged form.

The least that can be said is that bourgeois democracy was not reinvigorated by the crushing defeat of fascism. In any event, it had made the latter's bed and showed itself incapable of standing in its way. It no longer has a doctrine or any faith in itself. It has not succeeded in restoring its image by capturing for its benefit the fervor of the French popular masses against Hitlerism. The Resistance lost its raison d'être on the day its enemy disappeared. Its false unity immediately disintegrated. Its myth was deflated. The politicians of the postwar period were the most pitiful we have ever endured. They themselves vaporized the overly credulous confidence of those who, for want of anything better, turned to London against Vichy.[2] Bourgeois democracy showed itself to be totally incapable of resolving the problems and contradictions of the postwar period, contradictions even more insoluble than they were before the so-called crusade undertaken to find a solution to them. It was only able to survive at home through a shameful and hypocritical caricature of fascist methods, and abroad through colonial wars and even wars of aggression. It has capitulated. Its succession is open. And the anachronistic Fifth Republic was only able to put an ineffective band-aid on the wound, one more harmful than the previous medicines and, what is more, ephemeral.[3]

And then Stalinism, which claimed and which many believed to be made of sterner stuff and to be historically destined to substitute itself for the moribund (fascist or "democratic") forms of bourgeois domination, collapsed in its turn in the scandal of the ignominies revealed in Khrushchev's secret report, in the horrors of the Hungarian repression, and the invasion of Czechoslovakia.[4]

But a world that is collapsing is also a world being reborn. Far from allowing ourselves to fall into doubt, inaction, confusion or despair, the time has come for the French working-class movement to start again from zero, to rethink the very bases of its problems, to remake, as Quinet said, all of its baggage of ideas.

It was a concern of that order that, in the days following the Liberation, led me to go back to the French Revolution.[5] If my intentions were not clear enough and if as a result and through my fault, they escaped many of my readers and opponents, a British critic nevertheless understood: "Each generation must re-write history for itself. If the nineteenth century in Western Europe was the century of Liberty, the present century is that of Equality. The twin ideals of the French Revolution, so long separated by the political ascendancy of nineteenth-century Liberalism, are coming together again. This *rapprochement*, dictated by the course of events and the direction of the historical process itself, makes new demands on all who aspire to describe and interpret that process. If the twin ideals which Western civilization owes so largely to the French Revolution are to be again reconciled in action, they must surely be also—and perhaps first—reconciled in the description of their evolution by historians." And this anonymous critic found it "natural that when France is passing through a phase of political and economic reconstruction . . . she should seek guidance from a more many-sided social interpretation of her history." [6]

But in my opinion, the necessary synthesis of the ideas of equality and liberty that this critic recommended in far too vague and confused a fashion cannot and must not be attempted within the framework and for the benefit of a bankrupt bourgeois democracy. It can and should be within the framework of socialist (and communist) thought, which remains, despite it all, the sole solid value of our epoch. The dual failures of reformism and Stalinism place before us the urgent duty of reconciling proletarian democracy and socialism, freedom and Revolution.

And it was precisely the French Revolution that first provided us with the material for this synthesis. For the first time in history the antagonistic notions of freedom and coercion, of state power and the power of the masses confronted each other, clearly if not fully, in its immense crucible. From this fertile experience, as Kropotkin saw, emerged the two great currents of modern socialist thought on the basis of which we can remake our ideological "baggage" only if we finally succeed in finding the correct synthesis.[7]

The return to the French Revolution has, until today, been relatively fruitless, because modern revolutionaries, all of whom have nevertheless studied it closely and passionately, have only been concerned with superficial analogies, with formal points of resemblance with this situation, or that political group, or some other personality of their time. It would be quite amusing to recapitulate all these fantasies, sometimes brilliant, sometimes simply absurd, about which historians of the Russian Revolution like Boris Souvarine, Erich Wollenberg, and Isaac Deutscher were right to have reservations.[8] But we would need pages and pages to do this, and we have better things to do. If, on the other hand, we abandon the little game of analogies and attempt to get to the heart of the problems of the French Revolution and analyze its internal mechanism, we could draw lessons from it which would be extremely useful for understanding the present.

The Direct Democratization of 1793

The first thing to emphasise is that the French Revolution was the first coherent, wide-scale, historical manifestation of a new type of democracy. The Great Revolution was not simply, as too many republican historians believed, the cradle of parliamentary democracy: because at the same time that it was a bourgeois revolution it was also the embryo of proletarian revolution, it bore within itself the seed of a new form of revolutionary power whose features would become more distinct over the course of the revolutions of the late nineteenth and the twentieth centuries. The thread that runs from the Commune of 1793 to that of 1871, and from that to the soviets of 1905 and 1917, is clear.

I would here like to limit myself to briefly summarizing some of the general features of the "direct democracy" of 1793.

If we step into the "sections," the popular societies of the Year II,[9] we have the feeling of a reinvigorating immersion in democracy. The periodic self-purging of each "popular society," each candidate mounting the podium to offer him or herself to the scrutiny of all; the concern to ensure the most perfect possible expression of the popular will, to prevent its stifling by the golden-tongued or by idlers; permitting the working people to lay down their tools without any financial sacrifice and so to fully participate in public life; ensuring permanent control of the representatives by the represented; and the placing of the two sexes on a level of complete equality in deliberations.[10] . . . These are some of the features of a democracy truly propelled from the bottom up.

The General Council of the Commune of 1793, at least until the decapitation of its magistrates by the bourgeois central power, also offers us a remarkable example of direct democracy. The members of the Council were the delegates of their respective sections, constantly in contact with them and under the control of those who gave them their mandates, always up to date on the will of the base through the admission of popular delegations to the sittings of the Council. At the Commune there was no such thing as the "separation of powers" between the executive and the legislative. The members of the Council were both administrators and legislators. These modest sans-culottes did not become professional politicians; they remained the men of their professions or trades, still exercising them to the extent that their functions on the Commune allowed this, and ready to exercise them again at the end of their mandates.[11]

But of all these features the most admirable one is doubtless the maturity of a direct democracy experimented with for the first time in a relatively backward country, barely out of the night of feudalism and absolutism, still plunged in illiteracy and age-old habits of submission. No "anarchy," no confusion in this unprecedented and improvised management by the people. To convince oneself of this it is enough to leaf through the minutes of the popular societies, of the sittings of the general council of the Commune. There one can see the masses, as if aware of their natural tendency to indiscipline, animated by an ever present concern for self-discipline. They organize their deliberations and they impose order on those who might be tempted to provoke disorder. Even though in 1793 their experience of public life was relatively recent, even though most of the sans-culottes, guided it is true by educated petit-bourgeois, did not yet know how to read or write, they already demonstrated a capacity for self-management that even today the bourgeoisie, anxious to preserve its monopoly over public affairs, persists against all the evidence in denying. And certain revolutionary theoreticians, full of a sense of intellectual superiority, sometimes also tend to underestimate this capacity of the masses for self-government.

Direct Democracy and Vanguard

But at the same time the difficulties and contradictions of self-management made their appearance. The lack of education and the relative backwardness of their political consciousness were obstacles to the masses' full participation in public life. Not all of the people have a sense of their true interests. While some demonstrated extraordinary lucidity for the period, others allowed themselves to be led astray. The revolutionary bourgeoisie took advantage of the prestige it earned in its uncompromising struggle against the remnants of the *ancien régime* to inculcate in the sans-culottes a seductive but false ideology which in fact went against their aspirations for full equality. If we flick through the voluminous collection of reports from the secret agents of the Ministry of the Interior, we can see that informers reported comments made on the streets by men of the people, the contents of which are sometimes revolutionary, sometimes counter-revolutionary.[12] And these remarks are all lumped together and considered to be the expressions of the *vox populi* without any attempt to discriminate among them or to analyze their obvious contradictions.

The relative confusion of the people, notably of manual workers deprived of education, left the field open to better educated or more conscious minorities. This was how the Maison Commune Section, made up largely of masons, a small core group "got it to do whatever they wanted."[13] In many popular societies, despite all the care taken and the concern to ensure the most perfect functioning of democracy, factions led the dance in one direction or the other, and they sometimes even opposed each other.

The great lesson of 1793 is not just that direct democracy is viable, it is also that the vanguard of a society, when it is still a minority in relation to the mass of the country that it carries along with it, cannot avoid, in that life-or-death battle that is a revolution, imposing its will on the majority, first and preferentially through persuasion, and, if persuasion fails, by force.

It was in the experience of the French Revolution that Marx and Engels found the source for their famous notion of the "dictatorship" of the proletariat. Unfortunately, it was never truly elaborated by its authors. Without claiming, like Kautsky in the period when he was a reformist, that in their work it is nothing but a *Wörtchen*, a little word occasionally used but of no importance,[14] one is forced to say that they only ever used it too briefly and too vaguely in their writings. And when in particular they discover it in the French Revolution the terms they employ are far from clear and are debatable.[15] In fact, the revolutionaries of the Year II, convinced though they were of the need for exceptional measures, for having recourse to force, had a horror of using the word dictatorship. The Commune of 1793, like its heir of 1871, wanted to guide and not "impose its supremacy." Marat himself, the sole revolutionary of his time who called for a dictatorship, was forced to resort to careful language: he asked for a guide and not a master. But even in this veiled form he scandalized his brothers in arms and earned their loud protests.

Let it be understood: democracy had just issued its first cry. The tyrant had just been overthrown and the Bastille razed. The word "dictatorship" had a bad ring to it. It evoked the idea of a descent once again into tyranny, into personal power. In fact, for the men of the eighteenth century, nourished on memories of antiquity, dictatorship had a precise and formidable meaning. They recalled—and the *Encyclopedia* was there to remind them—that the Romans, "having driven out their kings saw themselves obliged, in difficult times, to temporarily create a dictator enjoying greater power than any enjoyed by the ancient kings." They recalled that later, the institution having degenerated, Sulla and Caesar proclaimed themselves perpetual dictators and exercised absolute sovereignty, in the latter case going as far as being suspected of having monarchist aims. They did not want either a new monarch or a new Caesar.

The men of 1793 had an even clearer memory of England. How could they forget that a century earlier Oliver Cromwell had overthrown an absolute monarch, usurped popular power, established a dictatorship, and even attempted to have himself crowned king? They feared a new Cromwell like the plague, and this was one of their complaints against Robespierre on the eve of Thermidor.[16]

Finally, the rank-and-file sans-culottes, the men and women of the popular societies, instinctively distrusted the word dictatorship, for it would have represented only a portion of revolutionary reality: they first of all wanted to convince, to open to everyone the doors to the nascent democracy, and they only resorted to force when those they wanted to convince and admit into democracy answered them with lead.

Perhaps they intuited that it is always an error to borrow words from the enemy's vocabulary. "The sovereignty of the people," as Henri de Saint-Simon pointed out, is one of those unfortunate borrowings. From the day they administer themselves the people are the sovereigns of no one. "The Despotism of liberty" (a phrase the men of '93 sometimes used in preference to "dictatorship" for it has a more collective resonance) and "dictatorship of the proletariat" are no less antonymic. The form of coercion that the proletarian vanguard finds itself forced to exercise against counter-revolutionaries is of so fundamentally different a nature from the past forms of oppression, and it is compensated for by so advanced a degree of democracy for the formerly oppressed, that the word dictatorship clashes with that of proletariat.

Such was the opinion of the libertarian collectivists like Bakunin, who were of course aware that the possessing classes would not voluntarily renounce their privileges and that they must be forced to do so, and who were determined to "organize a revolutionary force capable of triumphing over reaction"; but at the same time they categorically rejected any slogan of "so-called revolutionary dictatorship, even as a revolutionary transition," even if it is "revolutionary in the Jacobin manner."[17] As for reformists, they not only reject the words "dictatorship of the proletariat," but also what we have just seen defined as valid, namely the idea of revolutionary constraint or coercion. And so, for too long, Marxist revolutionaries have not dared to express any reservations concerning the words used, for fear of being suspected of "opportunism" regarding their essence.[18]

The inappropriateness of the terms appears still more clearly if we go back to the sources. The Babouvists (followers of Babeuf) were the first to speak of revolutionary "dictatorship."[19] Although they had the merit of drawing a clear lesson from the bourgeoisie's theft of the revolution, we know that they appeared too late, at a moment when the masses had surrendered. A minuscule and isolated minority, they doubted the people's capacity to lead themselves, at least in the near term, and they called for a dictatorship, either the dictatorship of one man or that of "hands wisely and resolutely revolutionary."[20]

The German communist Weitling and the French revolutionary Blanqui borrowed this concept of dictatorship from the Babouvists.[21] Incapable of joining up with a mass movement that was still embryonic, with a proletariat still too ignorant and demoralized to govern itself, they believed that small, bold minorities could seize power by surprise and establish socialism from above by means of the most rigorous dictatorial centralization, while waiting for the people to be mature enough to share power with their leaders. While the idealist Weitling envisaged a personal dictatorship, that of "a new messiah," Blanqui, more realistic, closer to the nascent working-class movement, spoke of a "Parisian dictatorship," that is, a dictatorship of the Parisian proletariat, though in his mind the proletariat was only capable of exercising this "dictatorship" in the person of one man, through the intermediary of its educated elite, of Blanqui and his secret society.[22]

Marx and Engels, though opposed to the Blanquists' minoritarian and voluntarist concepts, in 1850 made them the concession of adopting the famous formula,[23] going as far as identifying communism and Blanquism.[24] There is no doubt that in the minds of the founders of scientific socialism, revolutionary coercion seemed to be exercised by the working class and not, as in the case of the Blanquists, by a vanguard detached from the class.[25] But they did not differentiate such an interpretation of the "dictatorship of the proletariat" clearly enough from that of the Blanquists. Later Lenin, claiming to adhere both to Jacobinism and Marxism, would invent the concept of the dictatorship of one party substituting itself for the working class and acting in its name.[26] And his disciples in the Urals, taking his logic to its ultimate conclusion, frankly proclaimed, without being disavowed, that the dictatorship of the proletariat would be a dictatorship over the proletariat.[27]

From 1921 the German anarchist Rudolf Rocker, noting the "bankruptcy of state 'communism'" in Russia would maintain that the dictatorship of one class in and of itself is "absolutely unthinkable," and that in reality it is a matter of the dictatorship of one party claiming to speak in the name of a class. And he would forcefully rise up against the illusion of transforming the state, an organ of oppression, into an organ for the liberation of the oppressed, baptized "dictatorship" of the proletariat. "The state," he wrote, "can only be what it is, the defender of privilege and the exploitation of the masses, the creator of new classes and monopolies. Whoever does not know the role of the state does not grasp the essence of the current social order and is incapable of showing humanity the new horizons of its evolution."[28]

The Reconstituting of the State

The dual experiences of the French and Russian Revolutions teach us that we are touching upon the central point of a mechanism at the end of which direct democracy, people's self-management, gradually mutates, through the establishing of the revolutionary "dictatorship," into the reconstitution of an apparatus for the oppression of the people. Of course, the process was not exactly identical in the two revolutions. The first was that of an essentially bourgeois revolution, though already containing the embryo of proletarian revolution. The second was an essentially proletarian revolution, though having at the same time to fulfill the tasks of the bourgeois revolution. In the first case it was not the "dictatorship" from below, which had however already made an appearance, it was the dictatorship from above, that of the bourgeois revolutionary government, which provided the starting point for a new oppressive apparatus. In the second case it was from the "dictatorship from below," that of the proletariat in arms, for whom the party almost immediately substituted itself, that the oppressive apparatus was finally reconstituted. But in the two cases, despite this important difference, an analogy can be seen: the concentration of power, the "dictatorship," is presented as the product of necessity.[29] The revolution is in danger from both within and without. The reconstituting of the oppressive apparatus is invoked as indispensable for the crushing of counter-revolution.

Was the "necessity"—the counter-revolutionary danger—really the only reason for this abrupt turnabout? This is what most left-wing historians claim. Georges Lefebvre assures us that the Revolution could only be saved if the people were "organized and led by bourgeois cadres." It was necessary to bring together all the nation's forces for the benefit of the army. This could only occur by means of a strong and centralized government. Dictatorship from below could not succeed in this, since apart from the fact that it lacked the needed abilities, it could not forego an overall plan and a center of execution.[30] Albert Soboul considers that the direct democracy of the sans-culottes was, due to its "weakness," impracticable in the crisis through which the republic was passing. [31] Before them, Georges Guy-Grand, minimizing the political capacity of the popular vanguard, maintained that "the people of Paris did not know what to do with their riots. The riots were valid means of destroying, and destruction must sometimes be done. But demolishing Bastilles, massacring prisoners, aiming cannons at the Convention are not enough to make a country live. When cadres needed to be reconstituted, when industries and the government had to be made to function, there was no choice but to rely on the sole elements available, which were bourgeois."[32]

But it is not certain that the Revolution could only be saved by these techniques and from above. A relatively effective collaboration had been established at the base between the administration of staple goods and the popular societies, between the government and the revolutionary committees. The reinforcement of central power stifled and killed the initiative from below that had been the heart of the Revolution. Bourgeois ability was substituted for popular enthusiasm. The Revolution lost its essential strength, its internal dynamic.

What is more, we must be wary of those who invoke the pretext of "competence" to legitimize the exclusive and abusive use of bourgeois expertise during a revolutionary period. First, because men of the people are less ignorant, less incompetent than some people claim in order to make their case. Second, because the plebeians of 1793, when they were lacking in technical abilities, overcame that deficiency by their sense of democracy and their higher awareness of their obligations to the revolution. Finally, because the bourgeois technicians, reputed to be indispensable and irreplaceable, too often profited by their situation, which was considered impregnable, to intrigue against the people and to even develop suspicious ties with counter-revolutionaries. People like Carnot, Cambon, Lindet, and Barère were the agents of the great bourgeoisie and the sworn enemies of the sans-culottes. During a revolution a man lacking in competency but devoted body and soul to the people's cause, when he assumes civil or military responsibilities is worth more than a competent individual ready to betray.

During the six months or so of the flourishing of direct democracy the people demonstrated their creative genius; they revealed, though in a still embryonic form, that there exist other revolutionary techniques than those of the bourgeoisie, than one that is top-down. Certainly it is the latter that prevailed at the time, for the bourgeoisie had a maturity and an experience that conferred on it an enormous advantage over the people. But Year II of the Republic, if one knows how to decipher its message, foretells that the fertile potential of revolutionary techniques from below will one day win out in the proletarian revolution over the techniques inherited from the Jacobin bourgeoisie. Albert Mathiez, accustomed, as Georges Lefebvre admits, to "considering the Revolution from above,"[33] felt that he needed to draw an enthusiastic parallel between the "harsh" dictatorship of Public Safety of 1793 and that of 1920 in Russia.[34]

But even during the period when Mathiez was invoking the revolutionary bourgeois dictatorship of 1793 in an attempt to legitimize Lenin's Jacobin dictatorship, the German anarchist Rudolf Rocker supported the contrary thesis: "Referring to the French Revolution to justify the tactics of the Bolsheviks in Russia," he said, demonstrates "a total misunderstanding of historical facts. . . . Historical experience demonstrates the exact opposite: at every decisive moment of the French Revolution the true initiative in action rose directly from the people. The secret of the Revolution resides in this creative activity of the masses." On the other hand, it was when Robespierre deprived the popular movement of its autonomy and made it submit to central power, when he persecuted the authentically revolutionary tendencies and crushed the Left opposition, that the "ebbing of the Revolution, preface to 9 Thermidor and, later, to the Napoleonic dictatorship of the sword," began.[35] Rocker concluded with bitterness in 1921: "In Russia they are repeating today what occurred in France in March 1794."

The Embryo of a Plebeian Bureaucracy

Because the Great Revolution was not only bourgeois but was also accompanied by an embryonic proletarian revolution, one sees in it the germ of a phenomenon that will only assume its full scope in the degeneration of the Russian Revolution. Already, in 1793, democracy from below gave birth to a caste of parvenus differentiating themselves from the masses and aspiring to commandeer the popular revolution to their profit. In the ambivalent mentality of these plebeians, revolutionary faith and material appetites were closely intertwined. As Jaurès phrased it, the Revolution looked to them to be "both an ideal and a career."[36] They served the bourgeois revolution at the same time that they used it. Robespierre and Saint-Just, like Lenin in his time, denounced the appetite of this nascent and already invasive bureaucracy.

A certain number of them entered into open conflict with the Committee of Public Safety. If their attachment to bourgeois law and property flowed from their greed, they nevertheless had individual interests to defend against the revolutionary bourgeoisie. The latter, in fact, only wanted to leave them as small a piece of the pie as possible, first because that enormous budget-devouring plebs was expensive; second, because the bourgeoisie distrusted its origins among and its links to the people and, above all, the support from the working-class quarters which it had obtained demagogically with a view to occupying all posts; and finally because the bourgeoisie intended to keep the control of the revolutionary government in the hands of its tried and tested experts.

The struggle for power that opposed the plebeians to the experts was a sharp one and, in the end, it was settled by the guillotine. Certain important sectors such as the Ministry of War, the secret funds,[37] and the war industries were the stakes in this rivalry. The battle over the war industry was particularly revealing, for it was here that two modes of economic management confronted each other: free enterprise and what is today called state capitalism. If the plebeians had achieved their goals and if the war industry had been nationalized as they demanded, a portion of the profits coveted and finally seized by the revolutionary bourgeoisie would have gone into their pockets.

Trotsky, incompletely informed, is not totally correct when he asserts that Stalinism "had no prehistory," that the French Revolution knew nothing that resembled the Soviet bureaucracy, derived from a single revolutionary party and having its roots in the collective ownership of the means of production.[38] I think, on the contrary, that the Hébertist plebeians were, in more ways than one, a foreshadowing of the Russian bureaucrats of the Stalinist era.

In the same way, once the generals of the *ancien régime*, traitors to the revolution, were eliminated, there arose alongside the devoted but incompetent sans-culotte generals a new type of young chiefs risen from the ranks, capable but consumed by ambition and who would later be the instruments of reaction and military dictatorship. To a certain extent, these future Marshals of the Empire were the prefiguration of Soviet marshals.

"Anarchy" Deduced from the French Revolution

The French Revolution had hardly ended before "theoreticians" plunged into the analysis of its mechanisms and the search for its lessons with passionate ardor and an often remarkable lucidity. Their attention was concentrated essentially on two great problems: that of permanent revolution and that of the state. What they discovered first was that the Great Revolution, because it had been only bourgeois, had betrayed popular aspirations and had to be continued until the complete liberation of man. What they all deduced from this was socialism.[39] Some of them also discovered that within the Revolution a new type of people power, oriented from the bottom up, had made its appearance on the historical stage and that it had finally been supplanted by a powerfully reconstituted top-down oppressive apparatus. And they wondered with fright how the people could avoid seeing their revolution commandeered in the future. From this they deduced anarchism.

The first person who saw this, in 1794, was the Enragé Varlet.[40] In a short pamphlet written right after Thermidor he wrote this prophetic sentence: "For any reasoning being, government and revolution are incompatible." And he accused the "revolutionary government" of having, in the name of public safety, established a dictatorship.[41] "This is the conclusion," wrote two historians of anarchism, "that the first of the Enragés drew from 1793, and that conclusion is anarchist."[42] Varlet's pamphlet contained a profound idea: a revolution led by the masses and a strong authority (against the masses) are two incompatible things.

The Babouvists drew this conclusion in their turn. "The rulers," wrote Babeuf, "only make revolutions in order to continue governing. We want to make one to eternally ensure the people's happiness through real democracy." And Buonarotti, his disciple, foreseeing the commandeering of future revolutions by new elites added, "If there was formed within the state a class exclusively knowledgeable about the principles of the social art, laws, and administration, it would soon discover the secret of creating distinctions and privileges for itself."[43] Buonarotti deduced from this that only the radical suppression of social inequalities, that only communism would allow society to be rid of the scourge of the state: "A people without property and without the vices and crimes it engenders would not feel the need for the great number of laws under which the civilized societies of Europe groan."[44]

But the Babouvists were not able to draw all the consequences of this discovery. Isolated from the masses, they contradicted themselves, as we saw, by calling for the dictatorship of one man or of a "wise" elite, which would later lead Proudhon to write that "the negation of government, which shone briefly through the Enragés and the Hébertists before being snuffed out, would have issued from Babeuf's doctrines, if Babeuf had been able to think through the logical consequences of his own premise."[45]

It is Proudhon who, in 1851, had the merit of having drawn from the French Revolution a truly profound analysis of the problem of the state. The author of *The General Idea of Revolution in the Nineteenth Century* started with a critique of bourgeois and parliamentary democracy, of democracy from above, and of democracy by decree.[46] He denounced its fraudulent nature. He attacked Robespierre, an open enemy of direct democracy. He stressed the failings of the democratic constitution of 1793, a departure point, to be sure, but a bastard compromise between bourgeois democracy and direct democracy, which promised the people everything and gave them nothing and which, in any case, was no sooner promulgated than its implementation was indefinitely put off.

Getting to the heart of the problem, Proudhon declared, after Varlet, that "in proclaiming freedom of opinion, equality before the law, the sovereignty of the people, and the subordination of authority to the country, the Revolution made two incompatible things of society and the government." He affirms "the absolute incompatibility of authority with freedom." And he pronounced a fiery condemnation of the state: "No authority, no government, not even a people's government: the Revolution resides in this. . . . The government of the people will always be the swindling of the people. . . . If the Revolution allows government [the state] to survive somewhere, it will return everywhere." And he attacks the boldest of thinkers, the "authoritarian" socialists who, while admitting the misdeeds of the state "still said that while government is doubtless a scourge . . . it was still a necessary evil. "This is why," he adds, "the most emancipatory revolutions have always ended in an act of faith and submission to authority, why all revolutions have only served to reconstitute tyranny." "The people gave themselves a tyrant instead of a protector. Everywhere and at all times the government, however popular it was at its origin, after having shown itself to be liberal for a certain time, gradually became exceptional and exclusive."

He harshly condemned the centralization carried out through the decree of December 4, 1793.[47] This centralization was understandable under the former monarchy, but "under the pretext of a One and Indivisible Republic, to remove from the people the right to dispose of their forces, to call those who speak in favor of liberty and local sovereignty 'federalists' who are to be proscribed, means putting the lie to the true spirit of the French Revolution, to its most authentic tendencies. The system of centralization that prevailed in '93 was nothing but a transformed feudalism. Napoleon, who put the final touches to it, testified to this." Later, Bakunin, a disciple of Proudhon, would echo him: "A strange thing, that great revolution which, for the first time in history, proclaimed the freedom, not only of the citizen, but of man; but in making itself the heir of the monarchy it killed, it at the same time revived the negation of all freedom: the centralization and omnipotence of the state."[48]

But Proudhon's thought goes farther and deeper. He fears that the exercise of direct democracy, that the most ingenious formulas aimed at promoting an authentic government of the people, by the people—the fusing of the legislative and executive powers, the election and revocability of functionaries recruited by the people from within their number, and permanent popular control—that this system, which may be "irreproachable" in theory, "in practice encounters an insurmountable difficulty." In fact, even in this optimal hypothesis the risk remains of the incompatibility between society and authority. "If the entire people, as sovereigns, becomes the government, one seeks in vain where the governed would be. . . . If the people, organized as the authority, has nothing above them, I ask who is below?" There is no middle way, one must "either work or rule." "The people passing en masse over to the state, the state no longer has the least reason to exist, since there no longer exists a people: the result of the governmental equation is zero."

How to escape this contradiction, this "vicious circle"? Proudhon answers that the government must be dissolved in the economic organization. "The governmental institution . . . has its raison d'être in economic anarchy. Since the Revolution puts an end to this anarchy and organizes the industrial forces, there is no longer a pretext for political centralization."

The "Jacobin" Tradition

Bakunin in turn stresses that since their thought was "nourished" by a certain theory, which "was nothing but the Jacobin political system more or less modified for the use of revolutionary social-ists, the socialist workers of France never wanted to understand [that] when, in the name of the Revolution, you want to build a state, even if only a transitory state, it is a reactionary step and you are working for despotism."[49] To a certain extent the disagreement between Marxists and anarchists flows from the fact that the former do not always view the French Revolution in the same way as the latter. Deutscher saw that within Bolshevism there were two spirits, the Marxist and the Jacobin, a conflict that would never be resolved, neither in Lenin nor in Trotsky.[50] As we will see, there can be found within Bolshevism holdovers from Jacobinism more accentuated than in the original Marxism. But I think that Marxism itself never completely overcame an analogous contradiction. There is within it a libertarian frame of mind as well as a Jacobin and authoritarian frame of mind.

In my opinion, the origin of this duality can mainly be found in an at times correct, but also at times erroneous appreciation of the real content of the French Revolution. The Marxists see that the latter betrayed popular aspirations because it was, objectively and in its immediate results, a bourgeois revolution. But at the same time they are blinded by an abusive application of the materialist concept of history, which sometimes leads them to consider it only from the point of view and within the limits of the bourgeois revolution. Of course they are right to stress those relatively and inarguably progressive features of the bourgeois revolution, but there are moments when they present these features, which even anarchists like Bakunin and Kropotkin, if not Proudhon, exalted in a unilateral fashion, overestimating and idealizing them.

Because he was a Menshevik, Boris Nicolaevsky exaggeratedly stresses this tendency of Marxism. But there is something true about his analysis. And the German ultra-leftist of 1848, Gottschalk, was not completely wrong in balking at the Marxist perspective of "escaping the hell of the Middle Ages" only to "voluntarily leap into the purgatory" of capitalism.[51] What Isaac Deutscher says of the Russian Marxists prior to 1917—for, paradoxically, there was much "Menshevism" in these "Bolsheviks"—is also, I think, valid to a certain extent for the founders of Marxism: "Since they saw in capitalism an indispensable halfway house on the road from feudalism to socialism, they stressed the advantages of that halfway house, its progressive features, its civilizing influence, its attractive atmosphere and so on."[52]

If we examine the many passages in Marx and Engels concerning the French Revolution it has to be said that sometimes they see and sometimes they lose sight of its character as a "permanent revolution." To be sure, they do see the revolution from below, but only occasionally. To give an example, Marx does not hesitate to present the humble supporters in the working-class quarters of Jacques Roux and Varlet as the "main representatives" of the revolutionary movement, but Engels nevertheless writes that to the "proletariat" of 1793 "in its incapacity to help itself, help could, at best, be brought in from without or down from above."[53]

And so we can already understand better what Deutscher means by Jacobin spirit, namely the tradition of bourgeois revolution and dictatorship from above of 1793, somewhat idealized and insufficiently differentiated from compulsion from below. And by extension, we can understand the tradition of Babouvist and Blanquist conspiratorialism which borrows the dictatorial and minoritarian techniques of the bourgeois revolution in order to put them at the service of a new revolution.

One can see why the anarchists discern in the socialism and communism of the nineteenth century a certain "Jacobin," "authoritarian," "governmentalist" tendency; a propensity towards the "cult of state discipline" inherited from Robespierre and the Jacobins; that they define a "bourgeois frame of mind," "a political legacy of bourgeois revolutionism" to which they oppose the affirmation that the "social revolutions of our day have nothing or almost nothing to imitate in the revolutionary methods of the Jacobins of 1793."[54]

Marx and Engels deserve this reproach far less than other authoritarian and statist socialist currents of the nineteenth century. But they had some difficulty in freeing themselves of the Jacobin tradition. For example, they were slow in ridding themselves of the Jacobin myth of the "rigorous centralization offered as a model by the France of 1793." They finally rejected it, under the pressure of the anarchists, but not before having stumbled, hesitated, and modified their analysis and, even after all these corrective measures, they still went down the wrong road.[55] This wavering would allow Lenin to forget the anti-centralist passages in their writings—notably a clarification by Engels in 1885[56]—and to retain only "the facts cited by Engels concerning the centralized French Republic from 1792 to 1799," and to baptize Marx a "centralist."[57]

Indeed, the Jacobin hold was much stronger on the Russian Bolsheviks than it was on the founders of Marxism. And in large part this deviation has its origin in an occasionally incorrect and one-sided interpretation of the French Revolution. Lenin, it is true, clearly saw its permanent revolution aspects. He demonstrated that the popular movement, which he incorrectly called a "bourgeois democratic revolution," was far from reaching its objectives in 1794, and that it would only succeed in doing so in 1871.[58] If total victory was not won at the end of the eighteenth century, it was because "the material bases for socialism" were still lacking.[59] The bourgeois regime is only progressive in relation to the autocracy that precedes it, as the final form of domination and "the most fitting arena for the struggle of the proletariat against the bourgeoisie."[60] Only the proletariat is capable of pushing the revolution to its final end, "for it goes much further than the democratic revolution."[61]

But Lenin long rejected the concept of permanent revolution and maintained that the Russian proletariat, after the conquest of power, had to voluntarily limit itself to the bourgeois democratic regime. This is why he often tends to overestimate the heritage of the French Revolution, affirming that it will remain "perhaps for all time the model for certain revolutionary methods," and that the historians of the proletariat should see in Jacobinism "one of the culminating points that the oppressed class reached in the struggle for its emancipation, [one of the] best examples of democratic revolution."[62] This is why he idealized Danton[63] and did not hesitate to proclaim himself "Jacobin."[64] This is why, with much exaggeration, he attributes to bourgeois revolutionaries radical measures against the capitalists and claimed to act, like them, with "Jacobin inflexibility."[65]

Lenin's Jacobin attitudes brought him a sharp reply from Trotsky in 1904. For the latter, who had not yet become a Bolshevik, Jacobinism "is the maximum degree of radicalism that bourgeois society can provide." Modern revolutionaries must protect themselves from Jacobinism as much as from reformism. Jacobinism and proletarian socialism are "two molds, two doctrines, two tactics, two psychologies separated by an abyss." If both are intransigent, their intransigence is qualitatively different. The attempt to introduce Jacobin methods into the proletarian revolutions of the twentieth century is nothing but opportunism. Just like reformism, it is the expression of "a tendency to tie the proletariat to an ideology, a tactic, and finally a psychology foreign and hostile to its class interests."[66]

Towards a Synthesis

In conclusion, the French Revolution was the source of two great currents of socialist thought which, across the twentieth century, have lasted until today: an authoritarian Jacobin current and a libertarian current. One, of a "bourgeois disposition," oriented from the top down, is above all concerned with revolutionary effectiveness and claims to be taking account of "necessities." The other, of an essentially proletarian spirit, is oriented from the bottom up, and places the safeguarding of freedom to the fore. Between these two currents numerous more or less shaky compromises have already been elaborated.

Bakunin's anarchist collectivism attempted to reconcile Proudhon and Marx. Within the First International, Marxism sought a middle way between Blanqui and Bakunin. The Commune of 1871 was an empirical synthesis of Jacobinism and federalism. Lenin himself, in *State and Revolution*, was torn between anarchism and state "communism," between mass spontaneity and Jacobin iron discipline. Yet the real synthesis of these two currents is still to be effected. As H.E. Kaminski wrote, it is not only necessary, it is inevitable: "History itself constructs its compromises."[67] The degeneration of the Russian Revolution and the collapse and historical bankruptcy of Stalinism places it more than ever on the agenda. It alone will allow us to remake our "baggage of ideas" and to forever prevent our revolutions being commandeered by new Jacobins utilizing tanks, in comparison with which the guillotine of 1793 will look like a toy.

[1956, in *Jeunesse du Socialisme Libertaire*]

Notes

1. "Nous avons perdu nos bagages." Edgar Quinet, *La Révolution* (Editions Lacroix, Vanoeckhoven & Cie, 1869 [1865]), vol. I, p. 8. [Quinet was a prominent republican writer and historian. —DB]
2. 'Vichy' is shorthand for the quasi-fascist, collaborationist 'French State' created in 1940 under Marshal Pétain with its capital in the southern spa

town of Vichy (the northern half of the country, including Paris, having been occupied by German forces). [DB]

3. France's postwar Fourth Republic (1946–1958) was notorious for its political instability and inability to resolve the Algerian war of independence; it finally collapsed in 1958 under pressure from a generals' putsch in Algiers, and General Charles de Gaulle was made head of the government (and later president). The Fifth Republic, which he created, saw a reduction in the powers of parliament, a reinforced executive and the creation of a semi-presidential regime, widely perceived at the time on the left (including by Guérin) as being Bonapartist or quasi-fascist. Today there are still widespread calls for its democratization or even for the creation of a Sixth Republic. [DB]

4. The Hungarian Revolution of 1956 and the Prague Spring of 1968 were both crushed by Soviet bloc tanks. Both events led to a haemorrhage of members from Western Communist Parties. [DB]

5. *La lutte de classes sous la Première République, 1793–1797* (Paris: Gallimard, 1946; revised edition 1968), 2 vols.

6. *Times Literary Supplement*, 15 November 1947. [Guérin's text incorrectly gave the year of publication as 1946. He also failed to notice that the author's name was given in the contents page: Professor David Thomson. —DB]

7. See Kropotkin's *The Great French Revolution, 1789–1793*, first published as *La Grande Révolution, 1789–1793* (Paris: Stock, 1909). Most historians of socialist thought have failed to emphasise adequately the fact that these currents of thought were not simply born in the minds of the nineteenth-century ideologists (themselves the heirs of the *philosophes* of the eighteenth century), but from the lived experience of class struggles, in particular that of 1793. This gap is particularly evident in the chapter on the French Revolution with which the late lamented G.D.H. Cole opened his monumental history of socialist thought (*A History of Socialist Thought*, vol. I, 1953, pp. 11–2).

8. Boris Souvarine, *Staline* (Editions Champs Libre, 1977 [1935]), p. 265; Erich Wollenberg, *The Red Army* (London, 1970), pp. 78–80; Isaac Deutscher, *Staline* (Gallimard, 1953), p. 7.

9. As part of a broader move to do away with everything related to the pre-revolutionary regime and the reactionary influence of the Catholic Church, a new Republican calendar, with months named after seasonal aspects of the natural world, was instituted. 'Year I' began after the declaration of the Republic in 1792. The calendar was later abolished by Napoleon, but taken up again very briefly during the Paris Commune of 1871. [DB]

10. See, amongst others, Marc-Antoine Jullien in the "Société populaire" of La Rochelle, 5 March 1793, in Edouard Lockroy, *Une mission en Vendée, 1793* (Paris: Paul Ollendorf éditeur, 1893), pp. 245–8, quoted in Daniel Guérin, *La lutte de classes*, vol. I, pp. 177–8.

11. See Paul Sainte-Claire Deville, *La Commune de l'an II* (Paris: Plon, 1946).

12. Pierre Caron, *Paris pendant la Terreur* (Paris: Alphonse Picard, 1910–1964), 6 vols.

13. In Pierre Caron, *Paris pendant la Terreur*, vol. 6 ("observer" Boucheseiche, 29 March 1794).

14. Karl Kautsky, *Die Diktatur des Proletariats* (Vienna 1918); published as *The Dictatorship of the Proletariat* in 1919 (National Labour Press) [DB]. See also his *Materialistische Geschichtsauffassung* (1927), vol. II, p. 469. Cf. Lenin's *The Proletarian Revolution and the Renegade Kautsky* (1918).

15. Thus in his critique of the Erfurt Programme, Engels wrote that the democratic republic was "the specific form for the dictatorship of the proletariat, as the Great French Revolution has already shown." 'A Critique of the Draft Social-Democratic Program of 1891', *Marx-Engels Complete Works*, vol. 27, p. 217.

16. When Saint-Just proposed the concentration of power in the hands of Robespierre, the idea of a personal dictatorship caused a furore among his colleagues, and Robert Lindet exclaimed: "We did not make the Revolution in order to benefit one individual." In Armand Montier, *Robert Lindet* (1899), p. 249. [Thermidor was a month in the revolutionary calendar, and 9 Thermidor Year II was the date of the overthrow of Robespierre and the Jacobins; "Thermidor" has thus come to be shorthand for counter-revolution. —DB]

17. Bakunin, article in *L'Egalité* (26 June 1869) reproduced as an appendix in *Mémoire de la Fédération jurassienne* (Sonvillier, 1873); *Œuvres* (Stock), vol. IV, p. 344; 'Programme de l'Organisation révolutionnaire des Frères internationaux', in *L'Alliance internationale de la démocratie socialiste et l'Association internationale des travailleurs* (London & Hamburg, 1873). It is true that Bakunin, when under the influence of the Blanquists, would occasionally use the word "dictatorship", but he would always pull himself back immediately: "dictatorship, but not one sanctioned by the officer's sash, governmental title or legal institution, and all the more powerful for having none of the accoutrements of power" (Letter to Albert Richard, 1870, in Richard, *Bakounine et l'Internationale à Lyon*. Cf. also Fritz Brupbacher, 'Soixante ans d'hérésie' in *Socialisme et Liberté* (Editions de la Baconnière Boudry, 1955), p. 259.

18. They shook with fear at the thought of contradicting Lenin, for whom anyone who did not understand the necessity of dictatorship had understood nothing about the Revolution and could therefore not be a true revolutionary. See his 'Contribution à l'histoire de la dictature' (1920), in V.I. Lenin, *De l'Etat* (Paris: Bureau d'éditions, 1935).

19. Gracchus Babeuf (1760–1797), guillotined for his part in the Conspiracy of the Equals, was widely influential in the nineteenth century and is

regarded as a precursor of revolutionary socialism. See Ian Birchall, *The Spectre of Babeuf* (Chicago: Haymarket Books, 2016). [DB]

20. Philippe Buonarotti, *Conspiration pour l'égalité, dite de Babeuf* (Librairie romantique, 1828), vol. I, pp. 93, 134, 139, 140. [*History of Babeuf's 'Conspiracy of Equals'* —DB]

21. Wilhelm Weitling (1808–1871), a Prussian tailor, lived in Paris from 1837 to 1841 and was influenced by Charles Fourier, Robert Owen, Etienne Cabet and early millenarian Christian movements. A member of the communist League of the Just, he was admired by many leading revolutionaries of the time, including Marx and Bakunin. [DB]

22. Kautsky, *The Dictatorship of the Proletariat*; Preface by V.P. Volguine in Albert Soboul, Pierre Angrand and Jean Dauty (eds.), *Textes choisis de Blanqui* (Paris: Editions sociales, 1955), pp. 20 and 41; Maurice Dommanget, *Les idées politiques et sociales d'Auguste Blanqui* (Paris: Librairie Marcel Rivière, 1957), pp. 170–3.

23. Cf. *Les Cahiers du bolchevisme*, 14 March 1933, p. 451.

24. Marx, *La Lutte de classes en France* [1850] (Ed. Schleicher, 1900), p. 147. ["The *proletariat* rallies more and more around *revolutionary socialism*, around *communism*, for which the bourgeoisie has itself invented the name of *Blanqui*. This socialism is the *declaration of the permanence of the revolution*, the *class dictatorship* of the proletariat as the necessary transit point to the *abolition of class distinctions generally*" —Marxists Internet Archive. DB]

25. Maximilien Rubel, *Karl Marx, pages choisies pour une éthique socialiste* (Paris: Marcel Rivière, 1948), pp. 224–5.

26. A reference to Lenin's comment: "A Jacobin who wholly identifies himself with the organisation of the proletariat—a proletariat conscious of its class interests—is a revolutionary Social Democrat." (Collected Works 7: p. 383) Rosa Luxemburg challenges this claim in her 'Organizational Questions of the Russian Social Democracy', while Kropotkin stressed the fundamentally bourgeois nature and role of the Jacobins in *La Science Moderne et l'Anarchie* (Paris, 1913) and *The Great French Revolution, 1789–1793* (1909). [DB]

27. Cf. Léon Trotski, *Nos tâches politiques* [1904], notably the final chapter entitled 'Dictature sur le prolétariat'.

28. *Der Bankrott des russischen Staatskommunismus* (Berlin, 1921), pp. 28–31; published in French as *Les soviets trahis par les bolcheviks* (Spartacus, 1973, new edition 1998). [This text, whose title means "The Bankruptcy of Russian State-Communism", does not seem to have been translated into English. DB]

29. Cf. Proudhon, *Idée générale de la Révolution* (1851) in *Œuvres complètes* (Paris: Rivière, 1926), pp. 121–6; Deutscher, *Staline*, pp. 8–9.

30. Georges Lefebvre, *Annales historiques* . . . April–June 1947, p. 175.

31. Albert Soboul, 'Robespierre and the Popular Movement of 1793–1794' in *Past and Present* (May 1954), p. 60.

32. Georges Guy-Grand, *La Démocratie et l'après-guerre* (Paris: Garnier, 1920), p. 230.

33. Georges Lefebvre, *Etudes sur la Révolution française* (Paris: PUF, 1954), p. 21.

34. Albert Mathiez, *L'Humanité*, 19 August 1920; quoted in Guy-Grand, op. cit., p. 225.

35. *Der Bankrott*, op. cit.

36. Jean Jaurès (1859–1914), a schoolteacher and university lecturer turned politician, was one of the principal figures in the history of French socialism. Initially a left-wing republican, he was instrumental in creating and became the leader of the French Socialist Party (opposed to the Socialist Party of France led by the self-proclaimed Marxist Jules Guesde), and in 1904 he founded the newspaper *L'Humanité* (which from 1920 would be the paper of the French Communist Party). In 1905, the two socialist parties merged to create the Unified Socialist Party, French Section of the Workers' International (PSU-SFIO). Because of his outspoken pacifism, Jaurès was assassinated by a nationalist in 1914 shortly before the outbreak of war. [DB]

37. The Ministry of War used the *fonds secrets* (secret funds) to fund intelligence activities. [DB]

38. Trotsky, *Staline* (Paris: UGE, 1979 [1948]), pp. 485, 556–60.

39. The expression "permanent revolution" can be found in the writings of Bakunin as well as in those of Blanqui and Marx. [See also Proudhon's 'Toast to the Revolution', 17 October 1848: "From this it follows that revolution is always in history and that, strictly speaking, there are not several revolutions, but only one permanent revolution." In *Property Is Theft!*, p. 359 —DB]

40. Jean-François Varlet (1764–1837) was a supporter of the sans-culotte Hébert and was imprisoned more than once for his insurrectionism. [DB]

41. Varlet, *L'Explosion*, 15 Vendémiaire, Year III.

42. Alain Sergent and Claude Harmel, *Histoire de l'Anarchie* (Le Portulan, 1949), p. 82. (Republished by Editions Champ Libre in 1984.)

43. Born into the Italian nobility, Philippe Buonarroti (1761–1837) went to France in 1793 and was granted French citizenship for his services to the Revolution. He met Babeuf in prison after Thermidor and became a follower. Buonarotti's *History of Babeuf's 'Conspiracy of Equals'* (1828) was very influential. [DB]

44. Babeuf, *Tribun du peuple*, II, 294, 13 April 1796; Buonarroti, op. cit., pp. 264–6.

45. Proudhon, *Idée générale*, p. 195.

46. Ibid., pp. 177–236.

47. The decree of 14 Frimaire, Year II (by the revolutionary calendar) strengthened the power of the central authorities in Paris (especially the Committee of Public Safety and the Committee of General Security) and reduced those of local authorities. [MA & DB]

48. Bakunin, *Œuvres*, vol. I, p. 11.

49. Bakunin, *Œuvres*, vol. II, pp. 108 and 232. It was the same for the German socialists: Rudolf Rocker emphasised (in his *Johann Most*, Berlin, 1924, p. 53) how Wilhelm Liebknecht, the co-founder with August Bebel of the Social

Democratic Workers' Party of Germany, was "influenced by the ideas of the old communist Jacobins."

50. Trotski, op. cit., p. 95

51. Boris Nicolaevsky, *Karl Marx* (Paris: Gallimard, 1937), pp. 146 and 158. [Nicolaevsky (1887–1966) was a Marxist revolutionary and member of the Russian Social Democratic Labor Party. A prominent Menshevik intellectual, he was deported from the USSR in 1922 and settled for a time in Amsterdam where he became director of the International Institute for Social History. His *Karl Marx: Man and Fighter* was first published in German in 1933 and translated into English in 1936. —DB]

52. Deutscher, *Stalin: A Political Biography* (Oxford University Press, 1967), p. 30. Cf. also John Maynard, *Russia in Flux: Before October* (New York: Macmillan, 1955), p. 118.

53. Marx in ch. 6 of *The Holy Family* (1845), available on the Marxists Internet Archive at https://www.marxists.org/archive/marx/works/1845/holy-family/; Engels, *Anti-Dühring*, translation from Marxists Internet Archive: https://www.marxists.org/archive/marx/works/1877/anti-duhring/ch23.htm.

54. Proudhon, *Idée générale*, pp. 254–323; Bakunin, *Œuvres*, vol. II, pp. 108, 228, 296, 361–2; vol. VI, p. 257.

55. Engels, *Karl Marx devant les jurés de Cologne* (Ed. Costes, 1939), p. 247 and note; Marx, *Le Dix-Huit Brumaire de Louis-Bonaparte* (Ed. Scleicher frères, 1900), pp. 342–4; Marx, *La Guerre civile*, pp. 16, 46, 49; Engels, *Critique du programme d'Erfurt*, op. cit.

56. See the note by Engels in the 1885 edition of Marx's 'Address of the Central Committee to the Communist League' where Marx proclaimed that workers "must not only strive for a single and indivisible German republic, but also within this republic for the most determined centralisation of power in the hands of the state authority." Engels noted that "this passage is based on a misunderstanding" and that it was now "a well-known fact that throughout the whole [Great French] revolution ... the whole administration of the departments, arrondissements and communes consisted of authorities elected by the respective constituents themselves, and that these authorities acted with complete freedom within general state laws [and] that precisely this provincial and local self-government ... became the most powerful lever of the revolution." (*The Marx-Engels Reader* [New York: W.W. Norton & Co, 1978], pp. 509–10) [DB]

57. Lenin, *State and Revolution* (1917).

58. Lénine, *Pages choisies* (Bureau d'édition, 1926–7), vol. II, pp. 372–3.

59. Lénine, *Œuvres*, (First edition), vol. XX, p. 640.

60. Lenin, *Pages choisies*, vol. II, p. 93.

61. Lenin, *Pages choisies*, vol. II, pp. 115–6.

62. Lenin, *Pages choisies*, vol. II, p. 296; *Œuvres*, vol. XX, p. 640.

63. Lenin, *Pages choisies*, vol. III, p. 339.

64. Lenin, *Œuvres*, vol. XX, p. 640; *Pages choisies*, vol. I, p. 192.

65. Lenin, *Œuvres*, vol. XXI, pp. 213, 227, 232.

66. Trotsky, *Nos tâches politiques*, p. 66.

67. H.-E. Kaminski, *Bakounine, La vie d'un révolutionnaire* (Paris: Aubier, 1938), p. 17. [Republished by Editions La Table Ronde, 2003. Hanns-Erich Kaminski (1899–1963) was a socialist journalist originally from Eastern Prussia. He published a book about Italian fascism and campaigned for an alliance of the German Socialist and Communist Parties in the face of the Nazi threat. Having immigrated to Paris in 1933, he moved closer to anarcho-syndicalist circles and visited Barcelona in 1936. It was this experience which led to a book about the Spanish Revolution (*Ceux de Barcelone*, 1937) and the biography of Bakunin. In 1940 he immigrated to Argentina. —DB]

■ TWO INDICTMENTS OF COMMUNISM

Two books that appeared simultaneously, those of Tito's prisoner Milovan Djilas and Michel Collinet,[1] have led us to rethink the ideological foundations of Bolshevism. Even though produced by two men of different temperaments and origins and using quite divergent methods, they reach more or less the same conclusions and present more or less the same qualities, as well as the same defects.

One of their merits is to demonstrate that the Blanquist concept of the party formulated by Lenin from 1901 contained at least in germ the totalitarian communism of the Stalinist era. Djilas and Collinet stress that the ideological monopoly of the leadership of the party, in this case Lenin himself, claiming to embody the objective aspirations of society,[2] was in fact an idealist conception of history that would later result in the total monopolization of the bureaucratic apparatus over that society.[3]

Where the two writers diverge is on the historical excuse of "necessity." Djilas, still incompletely freed of the authoritarian concepts he was brought up on, believes that the success of the revolution, which had to defend its very existence and the indispensable industrialization of the USSR, required the establishment of a tyranny. Collinet, on the contrary, condemns Lenin for having made a virtue of necessity, and does not think totalitarian dictatorship necessarily flowed from the tragic circumstances of the Civil War.[4]

While establishing a direct connection between Leninism and Stalinism, the two authors stress, correctly, that under no circumstances can the two regimes be confused and that differences of an important nature distinguish them, and not simple "nuances," as Collinet once lets slip. Forms that were still revolutionary during Lenin's time were transformed into reactionary ones under Stalin.

Collinet and Djilas, in the most solid part of their work, provide both brilliant and implacable descriptions of the privileged "new class," of the feudal bureaucracy that seized power in the USSR. For Collinet today's Russian society realizes "the most perfect absorption of society by the state that history has ever seen," and for Djilas modern history has never recorded a regime oppressing the masses in so brutal, inhumane, and illegal a fashion. The methods it employed constitute "one of the most shameful pages of human history." And in a flight of inspiration, he opposes the idealism, devotion, and spirit of sacrifice of communism of its early days to the intolerance, corruption, stagnation, and intellectual decadence of contemporary communism. The analysis of the "new class," of the way it exploits the working class and its poor economic management, is more acute in Djilas than it is in Collinet: Djilas—and this is the main interest of his book—is a witness who lived the evil from within.

The two authors are in agreement in denouncing the thirst for and obsession with power of the communist oligarchs, as well as in stigmatizing the transformation of Marxism into a dogmatism, into an essentially sterile and conservative scholasticism.

Both Collinet and Djilas reproach Trotsky, not without reason and almost in the same terms, for having shown himself incapable, despite the great merit of his indictment of Stalinism, of defining sociologically and fully exposing the meaning of contemporary communism. Why? Because he lacked perspective, according to Djilas; because he persisted until his death in not questioning Leninist ideas of organization according to Collinet. There is probably something of the truth in both of these explanations.

But to my mind both books are marred by a certain number of errors I would like to point out.

In the first place, they both show a total lack of understanding of the concept of "permanent revolution." Collinet makes the mistake of considering Marx's famous text of March 1850 an unimportant accident in the history of Marxist thought, an ephemeral "Blanquist" crisis from which the author quickly recovered.[5] He and Djilas draw erroneous conclusions from a correct observation, which is that the "permanent revolution" is more acutely manifested in backward countries where it is easier to directly leap over the capitalist stage from feudalism to socialism. But they are wrong in concluding that revolutionary Marxism is only applicable to underdeveloped countries and that it has no chance in highly industrialized nations. Maintaining, for example, as Djilas does, that in a country like Germany only reformism can carry the day means forgetting that from 1918 to 1933 the German proletariat was on the brink of victory on several occasions and that without the errors caused by its being a satellite of Moscow, it would probably have abolished the most advanced capitalism of Europe. In May '68 did we not see the working-class revolt in France a hair's breadth from overthrowing an advanced capitalism?

What is more, the two books insist insufficiently upon the relatively progressive aspects of communism in power, although both mention some of them. Collinet accepts that the national bourgeoisies have been eliminated, the poor peasants liberated from the yoke of big landowners and usurers, and that industrialization has been carried out; Djilas that the collective ownership of the means of production has allowed for the realization of rapid progress in certain sectors of the economy. But the Yugoslav contradicts himself by claiming against all evidence that no great scientific discoveries have been made under the Soviet regime and that in this domain the USSR probably trails tsarist Russia. And in the final conclusions of these two books the progressive aspect is forgotten and the balance sheet presented is too negative.

In the same way, concerning the possibilities for the evolution of the post-Stalinist regime the two authors demonstrate a pessimism that in my eyes is excessive. To be sure, they are right in maintaining that the Khrushchev regime was that of a conservative pragmatism lacking in ideas. They are also right in stressing the relatively narrow limits of de-Stalinization and in being skeptical about the democratization and the decentralization of the regime, be it in Russia itself, Yugoslavia, or Poland. But at times when reading them it seems that "dialectical" evolution is blocked, that it forbids all hope. And yet, in other passages the two authors admit that the break with the Stalinist past is profound, that something has truly changed, that the domination of the "new class" has been shaken, that liberation is on the march, and that the release of popular discontent is irreversible. But they conclude that the outcome will be irremediable ruin and the collapse of "communism" without indicating with what the "monster" will be replaced.

An ambiguity all the more worrisome in that one senses in their analysis a singular indulgence towards Western bourgeois democracy, considered the sole alternative to "communist tyranny."

It seems that for both Collinet and Djilas the Russian regime alone is responsible for the Cold War and the division of the world into two blocs. The capitalist and imperialist character of the Western democracies is blurred. For Collinet financial capitalism is a "mythical monster," and even Djilas who has spent time in the U.S., contests the idea that the Western governments are controlled by a handful of monopolists. Collinet claims with a straight face that there exist Western democracies "untainted by any vestiges of imperialism," and Djilas that the United States tend towards an increasingly statist regime. The dangers that American big business and its claim to world leadership present are conjured away. Collinet goes even further when he attacks the Bandung Accords which, according to him, are "nothing but a weapon against the Western democracies," and when he presents Mossadegh and Nasser as instruments in the service of Russian expansionism.[6] The impact of the indictment of Stalinist totalitarianism and the executioners of the Hungarian people is considerably weakened by the blank check issued the aggressors of Suez and Western colonialism.

Why do Collinet and Djilas both go off the rails at the end of their analysis? In my opinion the real reason for their error is their inability to find a third way outside of those of Stalinism and bourgeois democracy. And the source of this inability is the refusal to rally to libertarian Marxist ideas.

They make only vague and insufficient allusions to the great conflict between authoritarian socialism and anarchist socialism that so deeply divided the working-class movement of the nineteenth century. They seem to be ignorant of the fact that the totalitarian communism they denounce was condemned a century before them in prophetic terms by Proudhon and Bakunin. For Collinet and even more for Djilas authority directly exercised by the proletariat in the absence of any state coercion is an "illusion" and a "utopia." And yet the two authors occasionally contradict themselves and express unconscious libertarian aspirations. Collinet lets slip that "the logic of democracy was not the Jacobin state, even animated by good intentions, but the state, withering away and transferring its functions to the entire social body." And Djilas, after having denounced the Jacobin-style intolerance of contemporary communists, exalts "man's imperishable aspiration for freedom," and announces as imminent the moment when industrialization will render communism "superfluous." Analyzing the demands of the underground opposition currently maturing in the USSR, Collinet—who is more precise than Djilas on this matter although, alas, he does not go as far as he should—says that "they do not appear to be demanding Western parliamentarism; rather their essence is the independence of the people and their economic and cultural organizations in relation to the party and state apparatuses."

If Collinet and Djilas had more clearly deduced these libertarian conclusions from their analyses they would have avoided getting bogged down, due to their failure to clearly glimpse a third way, in a pro-Western Menshevism that deprives their argument of much of its force and persuasive power. None of this, of course, justifies the prison sentence inflicted on the Yugoslav, which does no honor to Tito's regime.

The lesson: a revolutionary socialist who frees himself of Marxist-Leninist Jacobinism is in great danger of falling into petit-bourgeois and counter-revolutionary ideologies. There is only one healthy and certain way to "de-Jacobinize," to distance oneself from authoritarian socialism, and that is to go over to libertarian Marxism, the only reliable value of our time, the only socialism that has remained young, the only authentic socialism.

[1957, in *Jeunesse du socialisme libertaire*]

Notes

1. Milovan Djilas, *The New Class: An Analysis of the Communist System* (Thames & Hudson, 1957); Michel Collinet, *Du Bolchevisme: évolution et variations du Marxisme- léninisme* (Le Livre Contemporain, 1957). [Djilas, a former Yugoslav Partisan and Communist leader and at one point touted to succeed Tito as president, became increasingly critical of the Yugoslavian system and was imprisoned in 1956. *The New Class* had been finished before his arrest and was published in the USA in 1957, which led to his being sentenced to a further seven years' imprisonment. Eventually

released in 1966, he remained a dissident in Belgrade until his death in 1995. Collinet (1904–1977) was also a former Communist turned dissident, and then became a member of the Socialist Party's Revolutionary Left faction and, later, the Workers' and Peasants' Socialist Party alongside Guérin. He was active in the Resistance during the Second World War, and remained a member of the Socialist Party after the Liberation. —DB]

2. It is regrettable that neither Collinet nor Djilas quote the remarkable pages (pp. 157, 205) that, well before them, Voline, in his *Révolution inconnue*, dedicated to the Bolsheviks' claim to infallibility.

3. Nevertheless, Collinet and Djilas both exaggerate Lenin's dogmatic rigidity and underestimate his surprising intellectual flexibility and his ability to revise his positions in light of facts, aptitudes that on every occasion disconcerted his dull lieutenants and in a large measure compensated for the failing for which he is criticized.

4. Collinet here joins Voline without stating so (op. cit., pp. 180–2).

5. *Address of the Central Committee to the Communist League*, London, March 1850. [DB]

6. The Bandung Conference of 1955 brought together twenty-nine Asian and African countries, mostly former colonies, with the aim of promoting economic and cultural cooperation and opposing colonialism and neo-colonialism. Mohammad Mosaddegh was the democratically elected prime minister of Iran who was removed from power in a coup organised by British and US intelligence agencies in 1953. Gamal Abdel Nasser led the overthrow of the Egyptian monarchy in 1952 and nationalized the Suez Canal in 1956, which led to invasion by Britain, France, and Israel. [DB]

■ MAY, A CONTINUITY, A RENEWAL

With the exception of that by Cohn-Bendit, what is striking about some of the countless books written a tad too hastily about May '68 is the relative absence of references or insufficient references to the revolutionary past.[1] The books in which this omission can be found were written in general by young people. The young were the initiators of May and feel a legitimate pride in it. Through May, many discovered the Revolution, a Revolution that not all of them knew beforehand from books, or only knew it poorly due to the falsified versions that had been presented to them. From which a strange point of view develops which leads them to believe that in France everything began with May '68, that May was an absolutely original creation without any direct ties to French working-class and revolutionary traditions.

Claude Lefort displayed an illusion of this kind when in an article in *Le Monde*,[2] he boldly asserted that "with the May movement . . . something new is being announced . . . an opposition that does not yet know what to call itself, but which challenges the power structure in such a way that it cannot be confused with the movements of the past."

It is true that Lefort in this case was carried away by the ardor of a polemic against the various Trotskyist groups he reproaches, not without reason, with seeking to recuperate and monopolize the May movement at the risk of fossilizing it. But in making his case he exaggeratedly tips the balance in a direction opposite to that of the Trotskyist tradition, and I do not share his opinion that May is so radically different from the movements of the past.

To be sure, what is new, what is absolutely novel in May is that we witnessed the first act of an extended social revolution whose detonator was constituted not by workers, as in the past, but for the first time by students. Nevertheless, this peculiarity of May only concerns the first two weeks of the famous month, when it was the students who built the barricades and held the streets. The second phase of the "May revolution," the far more important one, that which more profoundly shook the political power and the bosses, which gave rise to the alarm of the property-owning class and the flight of their capital, was a revolution of the working class in the style and at the level of the great social crises of the past.

One wonders whether the reason certain people tend to overestimate the originality of the May revolution is that it arose during a historical stage when the Revolution had been emptied of all content in France; when it had been betrayed, perverted, erased from the map by two powerful political steam-rollers, two sterilizers of critical thinking: Stalinism and Gaullism. If May looked boldly anti-establishment, if it seemed to bring into question all established values and authorities as Claude Lefort seems to think, is it not because Stalinism for the last forty years and Gaullism for the past ten had caused the French to lose the habit of radical contestation, of libertarian protest? A habit, a taste, a tradition that had been theirs for almost 150 years.

Let us take the time to travel into our past and rediscover the countless May '68s of our national and social history.

For my part, scratching and digging behind the misleading façade constructed by bourgeois historians, I attempted to revive the mass movement of the revolution of 1793, extraordinary and unbelievable because it occurred in a France still more or less plunged in the darkness of absolutism, aristocracy, and clericalism. I followed step by step the bold incursions in the direction of the revolutions of the future dared by the sans-culotte vanguard, so far in advance of its time: the practice of direct democracy, the omnipotence of the power of the street. I compared, and how could one not, the Enragés of 1793 and those of 1968 by stressing this phrase of Jacque Roux, precursor of Daniel Cohn-Bendit: "Only the young are capable of the degree of ardor necessary to make a revolution."

When I had to describe the burst of vitality, of good sense, of good humor, more good-natured than cruel, that cast the people into the great adventure of de-Christianization in 1793 and led to the overturning of idols, I gave the chapter dedicated to this subject an expression borrowed from May '68: "All power to the imagination." For what we have here is the same creative genius.

All the social revolutions in France that followed that of 1793 and were born of its traditions were, like their predecessor, an exuberant festival of recovered freedom and an enormous collective release.

To a certain extent that was the case with the general strike in Paris in 1840, at the very moment when the idea of socialism was born in people's minds. This general strike is too little known, for here, too, the bourgeois historians, with the exception of Octave Festy, were no doubt superficial and negligent by design.

And what should we say about the tumultuous, fertile revolution of 1848, which bred so many ideas that emerged over several months from a popular crucible in turmoil, when so many public meetings and vast assemblies of the people where held, when so many newspapers, pamphlets, and tracts were born.

The libertarian explosion that was the Commune of 1871, the direct heir of that of 1793, was of the same kind. It is often hidden from us, or relegated to second place, by authors who have their eyes almost exclusively fixed on its civil war aspects. But during the short span of time when revolutionary Paris was able to blossom during a relative respite before it was subjected to the fatal aggression of the Versaillais, what a flowering, what an overflowing of joy and liberty! Armand Gatti, in the beautiful text he wrote in May '68 to comment on the projection of slides on the walls, perfectly grasped the parallels between "May '68" and the Commune.[3] Likewise, it would be giving a one-sided vision of the May revolution to reduce it to a series of street battles and to minimize the general contestation and the direct democracy. The confrontation with the CRS was the price that had to be paid to open the festival of freedom at the Sorbonne.[4]

The same libertarian impulse can be found in the great strike that followed the end of World War I in France just fifty years ago, combined with the mutinies of French sailors refusing to go to war with the Russian soviets. Do people know that on June 8, 1919, Toulon was the theater of a genuine insurrection, where sailors, soldiers, and workers fought shoulder to shoulder in the streets, stones in hand, against the gendarmes?[5]

For my part, I was fortunate enough, along with millions of other militants, to live through June '36, the immediate precursor to the workers' May '68. And along with all of them I can testify that France, paralyzed by the general strike and the factory occupations, and with the power of the masses master of the country, was on a par with the workers' uprising we lived through a year ago. Like the preceding explosions, the "revolution" of 1936 was an impressive festival of popular joy. Parades of millions of demonstrators filled the streets, just as on May 13, 1968. And in the factories, of which the workers had become masters, we participated in an immense popular festival, an enormous Bastille Day, one far more spontaneous than the one celebrated every year by the bourgeois republican tradition.[6]

Having participated in many debates in the lecture halls of the occupied university buildings in May, I can attest to the fact that the passionate and vibrant crowds that squeezed into them, far from turning their backs on the revolutionary past, were eager to find a continuity in it, to quench their thirst at that eternal spring of libertarian energy, which many of them had just discovered.

The rebirth of anarchism during May '68 might have seemed surprising. But looked at more closely, the French working class, and by extension the French people, has always retained an anarchist—or rather anarcho-syndicalist—substratum. Contrary to appearances, the CGT's tradition of class struggle and direct action which flourished from 1895 to 1914 never died. Many militants, and even leaders, who have since become Stalinist "Communists," have not completely succeeded in killing within themselves a repressed nostalgia for anarcho-syndicalism. The union split of 1921, the creation of the CGTU and then its Bolshevization did not cause the old syndicalist ferment to vanish from the consciousness of the workers.[7]

The general strikes of 1936 and 1968, both of which were accompanied by a wave of occupations, were spontaneous mass mobilizations of the rank and file, and were authentically anarcho-syndicalist.

Despite the maneuvers of counter-revolutionary bureaucrats like Georges Séguy,[8] the CGT of today in large measure remains, deep in its heart, anarcho-syndicalist, and that is what infuriates the aforementioned individual.

Finally, if anarchism was rediscovered in May, or rather entered into symbiosis with Marxism, there is no need to go far to find the cause: it is quite simply because at the moment that it blooms every social revolution can only be libertarian.

Only afterwards do the recuperators, the leaders who lay their paws on the Revolution, disfigure it and stifle it.

The revolution of May was aware of this danger. Up till now it has not succumbed. But beware!

[1969, in *Pour un Marxisme libertaire*]

Notes

1. *Le Gauchisme, remède à la maladie sénile du communisme* (Paris: Seuil, 1969). [In fact, the book—published in English as *Obsolete Communism: The Left-Wing Alternative* (Oakland: AK Press, 2001)—was coauthored by Daniel and his elder brother Gabriel. Daniel was associated with the anarchist group Noir et Rouge and was extremely critical of the Anarchist Federation; he became the figurehead of the revolutionary students' movement of May 1968. Gabriel was a member of the French Communist Party, but left it in 1956 and was associated with the Socialisme ou Barbarie group around Cornelius Castoriadis, as well as with other libertarian Marxist networks. DB]

2. *Le Monde*, April 5, 1969.

3. This seems to refer to Gatti's experimental play *Les 13 soleils de la rue St. Blaise*, produced by the Théâtre de l'Est Parisien. The award-winning poet, dramatist, and filmmaker Armand Gatti was born in 1924, the son of an Italian anarchist, and would take part in the armed resistance to Nazism. After the war he worked as a journalist for many years before he produced his first literary work and directed his first film. [DB]

4. The CRS (Compagnies Républicaine de Sécurité) are the French riot police, created in 1944. [DB]

5. Cf. 'Les Mutineries de la mer Noire', *Les Cahiers de Mai* (July 1969).

6. Commonly known in the English-speaking world as Bastille Day, 14 July has been the official French national celebration day since 1880, and marks not only the popular storming of the Bastille fortress, a symbol of absolutist monarchism, on 14 July 1789, but also the 'Festival of Federation' of 14 July 1790, which was organized by the supporters of constitutional monarchy and was intended to promote national unity in order to prevent any rolling back of constitutional changes and any further social conflict leading to more radical reforms. [DB]

7. The Confédération Générale du Travail (General Labour Confederation) was the first national trade union organisation in France, and before the First World War was strongly influenced by anarchism, leading to the

militant practice dubbed 'revolutionary syndicalism'. Increasingly moderate during and after the Great War, the movement split in the 1920s, with a Communist-dominated minority creating the CGTU (Unitary CGT). [DB]

8.   Georges Séguy had been a Communist Party (PCF) member since the 1940s and was general secretary of the CGT (which since the Liberation of 1945 had been dominated by the PCF) from 1967 to 1982. [DB]

■ SELF-MANAGEMENT IN REVOLUTIONARY SPAIN, 1936–1937

Self-management in revolutionary Spain is relatively little known. Even within the Republican camp it was more or less passed over in silence or disparaged. The horrible civil war submerged it, and still submerges it today in people's memories. It is not mentioned at all in the film *To Die in Madrid*.[1] And yet, it was perhaps the most positive legacy of the Spanish Revolution: the attempt at an original form of socialist economy.

In the wake of the revolution of July 19, 1936, the swift popular response to the Francoist coup d'état, many agricultural estates and factories had been abandoned by their owners. Agricultural day laborers were the first to decide to continue cultivating the land. Their social consciousness seems to have been even higher than that of the urban workers. They spontaneously organized themselves into collectives. In August a union conference was held in Barcelona representing several hundred thousand agricultural workers and small farmers. The legal blessing only occurred shortly afterwards: on October 7, 1936, the central Republican government nationalized the lands of "persons involved in the fascist rebellion."

The agricultural collectives gave themselves dual management, both union and communal, with the communalist spirit predominating. At general assemblies peasants elected a management committee of eleven members in each village. Aside from the secretary, all of the members continued to work with their hands. Labor was mandatory for all healthy men between eighteen and sixty. The peasants were divided into groups of ten or more, with a delegate at their head. Each group was assigned a zone of cultivation or a function in accordance with the age of its members and the nature of the task. Every evening the management committee received the delegates of the groups. They frequently invited the residents to a general assembly of the neighborhood for an account of their activity.

Everything was held in common, except personal savings, and livestock and fowl destined for family consumption. The artisans, hairdressers, and cobblers were grouped in collectives. The sheep of the community, for example, were distributed in groups of three to four hundred, entrusted to two shepherds and methodically distributed across the mountain.

Wage labor and, partially at least, money were abolished. Each worker or family received in remuneration for his labor a bond denominated in pesetas that could only be exchanged for consumer goods in communal stores, often located in churches or their outbuildings. The unused sum was credited to the individual's reserve account. It was possible to withdraw pocket money from this sum in limited amounts. Rent, electricity, medical care, pharmaceutical products, and old age assistance were free, as was school, which was often located in a former convent and mandatory for all children below fourteen, for whom manual labor was prohibited.

Membership in the collective was voluntary. No pressure was exercised on small landowners. They could, if they wished, participate in common tasks and place their products in the communal stores. They were admitted to general assemblies, benefiting from most of the advantages of the community. They were only prevented from owning more land than they could cultivate and one condition was posed: that their person or property not disturb the collective order. In most socialized villages the number of individuals who stood on their own, peasants or merchants, grew ever smaller.

The communal collectives were united in cantonal federations, above which were provincial federations. The land of a cantonal federation formed one holding, without boundary markings. Solidarity between villages was pushed to the extreme. Compensation funds allowed for the assisting of the least favored collectives.

From One Province to Another
Rural socialization varied in importance from one province to another. In Catalonia, a land of small and mid-sized property, where farmers had strong individualist traditions, it was reduced to a few tiny islands, the peasant union confederation wisely preferring to

first convince landowners by the exemplary success of a few pilot collectives.

On the other hand, in Aragon more than three quarters of the lands were socialized. The passage of a Catalan militia, the famous Durruti Column, en route for the north to fight the Francoists, and the subsequent creation of a revolutionary power issued from the rank and file, the only one of its kind in Republican Spain, stimulated the creative initiative of the agricultural workers. Around 450 collectives were formed, bringing together 600,000 members. In the province of Levante (its capital Valencia), the richest in Spain, some 600 collectives arose. They took in 43 percent of all localities, 50 percent of citrus production and 70 percent of its distribution. In Castile 300 collectives were formed with 100,000 members on the initiative of 1,000 volunteers sent as experts in self-management by Levante. Socialization also touched Extremadura and a portion of Andalucía. There were a few attempts at it in Asturias, but they were quickly repressed.

It should be noted that this socialism from the base was not, as some believe, the work of the anarchists alone. According to Gustave Leval's testimony, those engaged in self-management were often "anarchists without knowing it."[2] Among the latter provinces enumerated above, it was the socialist, Catholic, and in Asturias even Communist peasants who took the initiative in self-management.

When it was not sabotaged by its enemies or hindered by the war, agricultural self-management was an unquestionable success. The land was united into one holding and cultivated over great expanses according to a general plan and the directives of agronomists. Small landowners integrated their plots with those of the community. Socialization demonstrated its superiority both over large absentee landholdings, which left a part of the land unplanted, and over smallholdings, cultivated with the use of rudimentary techniques, inadequate seeding, and without fertilizer. Production increased by 30–50 percent. The amount of cultivated land increased, working methods were improved, and human, animal, and mechanical energy used more rationally. Farming was diversified, irrigation developed, the countryside partially reforested, nurseries opened, pigsties constructed, rural technical schools created, pilot farms set up, livestock selected and increased, and auxiliary industries set in motion, etc.

In Levante, the initiatives taken for the marketing of agricultural goods deserve mention. The war having caused a temporary closing of foreign markets and of the part of the internal market controlled by Franco, the oranges were dried; and wherever a greater quantity than previously was obtained, essence was extracted from the peel and orange honey, orange wine, medical alcohol, and pulp for the saving of blood from slaughterhouses for use to feed fowl was produced. Factories concentrated orange juice. When the peasant federation succeeded in reestablishing relations with French ports it ensured the marketing of agricultural goods through its warehouses, its trucks, its cargos, and its sales outlets in France.

These successes were due, for the most part, to the people's initiative and intelligence. Though a majority were illiterate, the peasants demonstrated a socialist consciousness, practical common sense, and a spirit of solidarity and sacrifice that inspired admiration in foreign visitors. Fenner Brockway of the Independent Labour Party, after a visit to the collective of Segorbe, testified to this: "The mood of the peasants, their enthusiasm, the way in which they made their contributions to the common effort, their pride in it, all of this is admirable."

The Sabotage of Self-management

However, there was no lack of difficulties. Credit and foreign commerce, by the will of the bourgeois Republican government, remained in the hands of the private sector. To be sure, the state controlled the banks, but it avoided putting them at the service of self-management. Lacking circulating funds, many collectives lived on what they had seized at the time of the July 1936 revolution. Afterwards they had to resort to makeshift methods, like seizing jewelry and precious objects belonging to the churches, convents, Francoists, etc. Self-management also suffered from a lack of agricultural machinery and, to a lesser degree, a lack of technical cadres.

But the most serious obstacle was the hostility, at first hidden and then open, of the various political general staffs of Republican Spain. Even a party of the Far Left such as the Workers' Party of Marxist Unification (POUM) was not always well disposed towards the collectives.[3] This authentically popular movement, the herald of a new order, spontaneous and improvised, and jealous of its autonomy, offended the machine of the Republican state as much as it did private capitalism. It united against it both the property-owning class and the apparatuses of the parties of the Left in power. Self-management was accused of breaking the "unity of the front" between the working class and the petit bourgeoisie and thus of playing into the hands of the Francoist enemy. Which did not prevent the detractors from refusing weapons to the revolutionary vanguard, reduced, in Aragon, to confronting the fascist machine-guns barehanded, and then to be attacked for "inertia."

On the radio the new Catalonian minister of the economy, Comorera, a Stalinist, incited peasants not to join the collectives, suggested to the small landowners that they combat them, and at the same time took resupplying from the hands of the workers' unions and favored private commerce. Thus encouraged from above, the dark forces of reaction increasingly sabotaged the experiment in self-management.

In the end, the government coalition, after the crushing of the "Barcelona Commune" in May 1937 and the outlawing of the POUM, did not hesitate to liquidate agricultural self-management by any means necessary. A decree dated August 10, 1937, pronounced the dissolution of the revolutionary authority in Aragon on the pretext that it "remained outside the centralizing current." One of its main inspirations, Joaquin Ascaso, was indicted for "sale of jewelry" destined, in reality, for procuring funds for the collectives. Immediately afterwards, the 11th Division of Commandant Lister (a Stalinist), supported by tanks, went into action against the collectives. The leaders were arrested, their offices occupied and then shut down, the management committees dissolved, the communal stores robbed, the furniture smashed, and the flocks dispersed. Around 30 percent of the collectives of Aragon were completely destroyed.

In Levante, in Castile, in the provinces of Huesca and Teruel, armed attacks of the same kind were perpetrated—by Republicans—against agricultural self-management. It survived—barely—in certain regions that had not yet fallen into the hands of the Francoists, notably in Levante.

Industrial Self-management

In Catalonia, the most industrialized region of Spain, self-management also demonstrated its worth in industry. Workers whose employers had fled spontaneously set to keeping their factories working. In October 1936 a union congress was held in Barcelona representing 600,000 workers with the object of socializing industry. The workers' initiative was ratified by a decree of the Generalitat, the Catalan government, on October 24, 1936. Two sectors were created, one socialist, the other private. The socialized factories were those with more than a hundred workers (those with between fifty and a hundred could be socialized at the request of three quarters of the workers), those whose owners had been declared "seditious" by a popular tribunal or who had abandoned its running, and finally those whose importance to the national economy justified their being removed from the private sector (in fact, a number of enterprises in debt were socialized).

The socialized factories were led by a management committee with between five and thirteen members, representing the various services, elected by the workers in a general assembly, with a two-year term, half of them to be renewed every year. The committee selected a director to whom it delegated all or part of its powers. In the key factories the selection of the director had to be approved by the regulatory body. In addition, a government inspector was placed on every management committee.

The management committee could be revoked either by the general assembly or by a general council of the branch of industry (composed of four representatives of the management committees, eight from the workers' unions, and four technicians named by the regulatory body). This general council planned the work and determined the distribution of profits. Its decisions were legally binding.

In those enterprises that remained in private hands, an elected workers' committee controlled the working conditions "in close collaboration with the employer."

The decree of October 24, 1936, was a compromise between the aspiration for autonomous management and the tendency towards state oversight and planning, as well as a transition between capitalism and socialism. It was written by an anarchist minister and accepted by the CNT (National Confederation of Labor), the anarchist union, because the anarcho-syndicalists participated in the Catalan government.

In practice, despite the considerable powers granted the general councils of the branches of industry, worker self-management risked leading to a selfish particularism, each production unit concerned only about its own interests. This was remedied by the creation of a central equalization fund, allowing for the equitable distribution of resources. In this way the surplus of the Barcelona bus company was transferred to the less profitable tram company.

Exchanges occurred between industrial and peasant collectives, the former exchanging underwear or clothing for the olive oil of the latter.

In the suburbs of Barcelona, in the commune of Hospitalitet, on whose borders farmers were involved in the planting of crops, the agricultural and industrial (metals, textile, etc.) self-managed organizations joined together in one communal authority elected by the people, which ensured the provisioning of the city.

Outside of Catalonia, notably in Levante, industrial self-management was experimented with in a few locations. This was the case in Alcoy, near Alicante, where 20,000 textile workers and steelworkers managed the socialized factories and created consumer cooperatives, as well as in Clastellón de la Plana, where the steel factories were integrated into larger units under the impetus of a technical commission in daily contact with each of its management committees.

But like agricultural self-management, industrial self-management faced the hostility of the administrative bureaucracy, the authoritarian socialists, and the Communists. The central Republican government refused it any credits, even when the Catalan minister of the economy, the anarchist Fabregas, offered the billions on deposit in the savings banks as a guarantee for the advances to self-management. When he was replaced in 1937 by Comorera the latter deprived the self-managed factories of the primary material they lavished on the private sector. It also neglected to ensure the deliveries ordered by the Catalan administration to the socialized enterprises.

Industrial Self-management Dismantled

Later, the central government used the pretext of the needs of national defense to seize control of the war industries. By a decree of August 23, 1937, it suspended the application of the Catalan socialization decree of October 1936 in the steel and mining industries, said to be "contrary to the spirit of the constitution." The former supervisors and the directors removed under self-management or, more precisely, who had not wanted to accept posts as technicians in self-managed enterprises, resumed their posts, with revenge in their hearts.

Catalan industrial self-management nevertheless survived in other branches until the crushing of Republican Spain in 1939. But industry having lost its main outlets and lacking in primary materials the factories that did not work for national defense were only able to operate with severely reduced staff and hours.

In short, Spanish self-management, hardly born, was restrained within the strict framework of a war fought with classic military methods in the name (or under cover) of which the republic clipped the wings of its vanguard and compromised with internal reaction. Despite the unfavorable conditions under which it took place and the brevity of its existence, which prohibits an evaluation and accounting of its results, the experiment opened new perspectives for socialism, for an authentic socialism, animated from the bottom up, the direct emanation of the workers of the country and the cities.[4]

[1984, in *À la recherche d'un communisme libertaire*]

Notes

1. A 1962 documentary by Frédéric Rossif. English-language films in which the collectivizations do feature include Ken Loach's *Land and Freedom* (1995); see also Mark Littlewood, *Ethel MacDonald: An Anarchist's Story* (2007), http://www.spanishcivilwarfilm.com. [DB]

2. Gaston Leval, *Espagne libertaire 36–39* (Éditions du Cercle/Éditions de la Tête de feuilles, 1971). [Published in English as *Collectives in the Spanish Revolution* (London: Freedom Press, 1975) —DB]

3. The POUM was formed by Andreu Nin and Joaquín Maurín in 1935 and was affiliated internationally to the so-called London Bureau alongside the ILP (Independent Labour Party) in Britain and the PSOP (Workers' and Peasants' Socialist Party) in France (of which Guérin was a prominent member at the time). [DB]

4. See Sam Dolgoff, *Anarchist Collectives: Workers' Self-management in the Spanish Revolution, 1936–39* (Montréal: Black Rose Books, 1975); Frank Mintz, *Anarchism and Workers' Self-management in Revolutionary Spain* (Oakland: AK Press, 2012). [DB]

■ LIBERTARIAN COMMUNISM, THE ONLY REAL COMMUNISM

It is time to outline a synthesis of all my work and attempt to sketch a program, at the risk of seeing myself accused of engaging in "metapolitics."

It would be futile to engage in a sort of replastering of an edifice of cracked and worm-eaten socialist doctrines, to struggle to patch together some of the surviving solid fragments of traditional Marxism and anarchism, to indulge in Marxist or Bakuninist scholarship, to seek to trace, merely on paper, tortuous connections.

If in this book we have often turned to the past it was of course not, as the reader will have understood, to dwell on it self-indulgently. To learn from it, to draw from it, yes, for previous experience is rich in teachings, but with an eye to the future.

The libertarian communism of our time, which blossomed in the French May '68, goes far beyond communism and anarchism.

Calling oneself a libertarian communist today does not mean looking backwards, but rather drafting a sketch of the future. Libertarian communists are not exegetes, they are militants. They understand that it is incumbent upon them to change the future, no more, no less. History has backed them against the wall. The hour of the socialist revolution has rung everywhere. Like the moon landing, it has entered the realm of the immediate and the possible. The precise definition of the forms of a socialist society no longer belong to the realm of utopia. The only people lacking in realism are those who close their eyes to these truths.

What will be the guiding lines that we are going to follow to accomplish the Revolution which, as Gracchus Babeuf said, will be the final one?

To start with, before going into action, libertarian communists assess the exact nature of objective conditions; they attempt to evaluate accurately the balance of power in every situation. Here the method elaborated by Karl Marx and which has not aged, namely historical and dialectical materialism, remains the surest of compasses, an inexhaustible mine of models and guideposts. On condition, however, that it be treated as Marx did himself, that is, without doctrinal rigidity, and that it avoid mechanistic inflexibility; on condition that, sheltering beneath its wing, one does not eternally invent poor pretexts and pseudo-objective reasons to excuse oneself from pushing things to the limit, to sow confusion, to miss the revolutionary opportunity every time it presents itself.

Libertarian communism is a communism that rejects determinism and fatalism, which gives space to individual will, intuition, imagination, the rapidity of reflexes, the profound instinct of the large masses, who are wiser at moments of crisis than the reasonings of the "elite," who believe in the element of surprise and provocation, in the value of audacity, who do not allow themselves to be encumbered and paralyzed by a weighty, supposedly "scientific" ideological apparatus, who do not prevaricate or bluff, who avoid both adventurism and fear of the unknown.

Libertarian communists have learned from experience how to set about things: they hold in contempt the impotent shambles of disorganization as much as the bureaucratic ball and chain of over-organization.

Libertarian communists, faithful on this point to both Marx and Bakunin, reject the fetishism of the single, monolithic, and totalitarian party, just as they avoid the traps of a fraudulent and demobilizing electoralism.

Libertarian communists are, in their essence, internationalists. They consider the global struggles of the exploited as a whole. But they nonetheless take into account the specificity and the original forms of socialism in each country. They only conceive internationalism to be proletarian if it is inspired from the bottom up, on a level of complete equality, without any form of subordination to a "big brother" who thinks himself stronger and cleverer.

Libertarian communists never sacrifice the revolutionary struggle to the diplomatic imperatives of the so-called socialist empires and, like Che Guevara, do not hesitate to send them both packing if their aberrant fratricidal quarrels cause mortal harm to the cause of universal socialism.

When the moment of the revolutionary test of strength arrives, libertarian communists will attack at both the center and the periphery, in the political and administrative fields as well as the economic. On the one hand, they will deal mercilessly, with all their might, and if necessary by means of armed struggle, with the bourgeois state and the entire complex machinery of power, be it at the level of the capital, the regions, the departments, or the municipalities; they will never make the mistake, on the pretext of "apoliticism," of neglecting, underestimating, or abstaining from dismantling the citadels, the political centers, from which the enemy's resistance is directed. But at the same time, combining the economic and political struggles, they will at their workplaces take control of all posts held by the bosses and wrest the means of production from those who monopolize them, in order to hand them over to their real, rightful owners: the self-managing workers and technicians.

Once that revolution is victoriously and completely accomplished, libertarian communists do not smash the state in order to reestablish it in another even more oppressive form through the colossal expansion of its capacities. Rather, they want the transmission of all power to a confederation of federations, that is, to a confederation of communes, themselves federated in regions, a confederation of revolutionary workers' unions preexisting the revolution or, failing that, the confederation of workers' councils born of the revolution, which does not exclude the eventuality of a merger of the latter two. Elected for a short mandate and not eligible for reelection, the delegates to these various bodies are controllable and revocable at all times.

Libertarian communists shun any particularist atomization into small units, communes, and workers' councils, and aspire to a federalist coordination, one which is both close-knit and freely consented to. Rejecting bureaucratic and authoritarian planning, they believe in the need for coherent and democratic planning, inspired from the bottom up.

Because they are of their time, libertarian communists want to wrest the media, automation, and computers from the maleficent monopolists and place them at the service of liberation.

Hardened authoritarians and sceptics maintain that the imperatives of contemporary technology are incompatible with a libertarian communist society. On the contrary, the libertarian communists intend to unleash a new technological revolution, this time oriented towards both higher productivity and a shorter work day, towards decentralization, decongestion, de-bureaucratization, dis-alienation, and a return to nature. They condemn the degrading mentality of the so-called consumer society while preparing to raise consumption to its highest level ever.

Libertarian communists carry out this gigantic overturning at the price of the least possible disorder, neither too slowly nor too soon. They know that a wave of the magic wand cannot instantly effect the most profound social transformation of all time. They do not lose sight of the fact that with the hominid distorted by millennia of oppression, obscurantism, and egoism, time will be needed to form a socialist man or socialist woman. They agree to transitions while refusing to see them perpetuated. And so it is that while assigning as the ultimate goal, to be reached by stages, the withering away of competition, the free provision of public and social services, the disappearance of money, and the distribution of abundance according to the needs of each; that while aiming at association within self-management of agriculturalists and artisans, at the cooperative reorganization of commerce, it is not their plan to abolish overnight competition and the laws of the marketplace, remuneration according to labor accomplished, small farming, and artisanal and commercial property.

They do not think superfluous the temporary assistance of active minorities who are more educated and conscious, whatever name they might give themselves, minorities whose contribution is unavoidable in bringing the rearguard to full socialist maturity, but who will not stay on stage one day longer than necessary and will merge as quickly as possible into the egalitarian association of producers.

The libertarian communists do not offer us yet another "groupuscule." For them the guiding lines that we have just laid out coincide with the basic class instinct of the working class.

In my opinion—and long, arduous, and painful experience has demonstrated this—apart from libertarian communism there is no real communism.

[1969, in *Pour un Marxisme libertaire*]

■ APPENDIX I

The Libertarian Communist Platform of 1971[1]

I—Individual and collective revolts punctuate the history of humanity, which is a succession of exploitative societies. In every era thinkers have arrived at an idea that calls their society into question. But it was with the advent of modern capitalist society that the division of society into two fundamental, antagonistic classes clearly appeared, and it is through class struggle, the motor of the evolution of capitalist society, that the road was constructed that leads from revolt to the achieving of revolutionary consciousness.

Today, because it has changed form, class struggle is sometimes denied by those who insist on either the bourgeoisification and integration of the working class, or the birth of a new working class that will supposedly insert itself naturally, as it were, into the decision-making centers of capitalist society. In fact, the old social strata are disappearing, the polarization into two fundamental classes is growing more acute, and there is always some spot in the world where the class war is being reignited.

Whatever the ideological forms it assumes, the capitalist mode of production is, globally, a unity. Whether it be in the form which, based originally on "liberalism," is headed towards state monopoly capitalism, or that of state bureaucratic capitalism, capitalism cannot but increase the exploitation of labor in order to attempt to escape the mortal crisis threatening it. Massacres, the general collapse of living conditions, as well as the exploitation and alienation peculiar to this or that human group (women, the young, racial or sexual minorities, etc.) are manifestations that cannot be separated from the division of society into two classes: that which disposes of wealth and the lives of workers, and creates and perpetuates the superstructures (customs, moral values, law, culture in general), and that which produces wealth.

The proletariat can today be defined broadly as follows: those who, at one level or another, create surplus value or contribute to its realization. Added to the proletariat are those who, belonging to non-proletarian strata, rally to proletarian objectives (such as intellectuals and students).

II—Class struggle and revolution are not purely objective processes, are not the results of mechanical necessities independent of the activities of the exploited. The class struggle is not simply a phenomenon to be observed: it is the driver that constantly modifies the situation and the facts of capitalist society. Revolution is its conclusion. It is the exploited taking into its hands the instruments of production and exchange, of weapons, and the destruction of the centers and means of state power.

To be sure, the class struggle is punctuated with difficulties, failures, and bloody defeats, but proletarian action periodically reemerges, more powerful and more extensive.

1. In the first instance it manifests itself at the level of direct confrontation in the workplace. It also manifests itself at the level of problems of daily life, in struggles against the oppression of women, the young, and minorities; in the questioning of education, culture, art, and values. But these struggles must never be separated from the class struggle. Attacking the state and the superstructures also means attacking capitalist domination. Fighting for better working conditions or wage increases means carrying on the same struggle. But it is clear that posing the problem of lifestyle, rather than just that of wage levels, gives the struggle a more radical aspect when this means the development of a mass movement demanding a whole new conception of life rather than merely quantitative improvements.

2. Historical analysis makes clear a profound tendency, expressed by the workers through their direct struggles against capital and the state, towards self-organization, and the structures of classless society appear embryonically in

the forms assumed by revolutionary action. The tendency towards autonomous action can be seen in the course of the most everyday struggles: wildcat strikes, expropriations, various forms of direct action opposed to bureaucratic leadership, action committees, rank-and-file committees, etc. With the demand for power at workers' general assemblies and the insistence on the revocability of delegates, it is true self-management that is on the agenda.

For us there is no historic and formal break between the proletariat rising to power and its struggles to achieve this, rather a continuous and dialectical development of self-management techniques, starting from the class struggle and ending with the victory of the proletariat and the establishment of a classless society.

A specifically proletarian mode of organization, "council power," arose during revolutionary periods like the Paris Commune (1871), Makhnovist Ukraine (1918–1921), the Italian workers' councils (1918–1922), the Bavarian council republic (1918–1919), the Budapest Commune (1919), the Kronstadt Commune (1921), the Spanish Revolution (1936–1937), the Hungarian revolt (1956), the Czech revolt (1968), and May '68.

The power of the councils, achieving generalized self-management in all realms of human activity, can only be defined through historical practice itself, and any attempt at a definition of the new world can only be an approximation, a proposal, an investigation.

The appearance and generalization of direct forms of workers' power implies that the revolutionary process is already quite advanced. Nevertheless, it should be presumed that at this stage bourgeois power is still far from being totally liquidated. And so a provisional dual power is established between the revolutionary and socialist structures put in place by the working classes and, on the other hand, the counter-revolutionary forces.

During this period the class struggle, far from being attenuated, reaches its climax, and it is here that the words class war take on all their sharpness: the future of the revolution depends on the outcome of this war. Nevertheless, it would be dangerous to view the process in accordance with well-defined norms. Indeed, the nature of state power (i.e., counter-revolutionary power) in its fight against the councils can take on different forms. What is fundamental is that council power is antagonistic to all state power, since it expresses itself within society itself through general assemblies, whose delegates in the various organizations that have been established are nothing but its expression and can be recalled at any time.

At this point authority and society are no longer separate, the maximal conditions having been realized for the satisfaction of the needs, tendencies, and aspirations of individuals and social groups, humanity escaping from its condition as object to become the creative subject of its own life.

And so it is obvious that the revolution cannot be made through intermediaries: it is the product of the spontaneous movement of the masses and not of a general staff of specialists or a so-called vanguard that is alone conscious and charged with the leadership and direction of struggles. When the word "spontaneous" is used here its use should not at all be interpreted as adherence to a so-called spontaneist idea privileging mass spontaneity at the expense of revolutionary consciousness, which is its indispensable complement and which surpasses it. In other words, an incorrect use of the notion of spontaneity would consist in likening it to a "disordered," "instinctive" activity that would be incapable of engendering revolutionary consciousness, as was claimed by Kautsky and later by Lenin in his *What Is to Be Done?*

It is no less obvious that the revolution cannot be a simple political and economic restructuring of the old society. Instead, by all at once overturning all realms through the smashing of capitalist production relations and the state, it is not only political and economic, but also at every moment cultural, and it is in this sense that we can utilize the idea of total revolution.

III—The real vanguard is not this or that group that proclaims itself the historic consciousness of the proletariat. It is, in fact, those militant workers who are at the forefront of offensive combat, and those who maintain a certain degree of consciousness even in periods of retreat.

The revolutionary organization is a place for meetings, exchanges, information, and reflection which enable the development of revolutionary theory and practice, which are nothing but two aspects of one movement. It brings together militants who recognize each other at the same level of reflection, activity, and cohesion. It can on no account substitute itself for the proletarian movement itself or impose a leadership on it or claim to be its fully achieved consciousness.

On the other hand, it must strive to synthesize the experiences of struggle, helping to acquire the greatest possible degree of revolutionary consciousness and the greatest possible coherence in that consciousness, which is to be seen not as a goal or as existing in the abstract, but as a process.

In summary, the revolutionary organization's role is to support the proletarian vanguard and to assist in the self-organization of the proletariat by playing—either collectively or through the intervention of militants—the role of propagator, catalyst, and revealer, and by allowing the revolutionaries that compose it coordinated and convergent interventions in the areas of information, propaganda, and support for exemplary actions.

A consequence of this conception of the revolutionary organization is its mission to disappear not through a mechanical decision, but when it no longer corresponds to the functions that justify it. It will then dissolve in the classless society.

Revolutionary praxis is carried out within the masses, and theoretical elaboration only has meaning if it is always connected to the struggles of the proletariat. In this way revolutionary theory is the opposite of ideological verbiage papering over the absence of any truly proletarian praxis.

What this means is that the purpose of the revolutionary organization is to bring together militants in agreement with the above and independently of any Marxist, anarchist, councilist, or libertarian communist label, the label serving to cover in fact the top-down and elitist understanding of the vanguard that is of course found among Leninists, but also among so-called anarchists.

The revolutionary organization does not exclusively invoke any particular theoretician or any preexisting organization, though recognizing the positive contributions of those who systematized, refined, and spread the ideas drawn from the mass movement. Rather it positions itself as heir of the various manifestations of the anti-authoritarian workers current of the First International, a current which is historically known under the name of communist anarchism or libertarian communism, a current which the so-called anarchist currents have, unfortunately, often grossly caricatured.

The revolutionary organization is self-managed. In its structures and functioning it must prefigure the non-bureaucratic society that will see the distinction between order-givers and order-followers disappear and that will establish delegation solely for technical tasks and with the corrective of permanent recall.

Technical knowledge and competencies of all kinds must be as widespread as possible to ensure an effective rotation of tasks. Discussion and the elaboration of ideas must thus be the task of all militants and, even more than the indispensable organizational norms, which can always be revised, it is the level of coherence and the consciousness of responsibilities reached by all concerned that is the best antidote to any bureaucratic deviation.

(This platform was discussed and adopted during a meeting held in Marseille on July 11, 1971. It had been called by the Mouvement Communiste Libertaire [MCL, Libertarian Communist Movement], founded by groups and individuals most of whom had come out of the former Fédération Communiste Libertaire [FCL, Libertarian Communist Federation], the Jeunesse Anarchiste Communiste [JAC, Communist Anarchist Youth], and the Union des Groupes Anarchistes-Communistes [UGAC, Union of Communist-Anarchist Groups] in the wake of May 1968 and within the framework of the fusion of several local groups of the Organisation Révolutionnaire Anarchiste [ORA, Anarchist Revolutionary Organization]. I actively participated in the discussion concerning its final version on the basis of a draft proposed by Georges Fontenis.[2] It was published in November 1971 in *Guerre de Classes* [Class War], newspaper of the Organisation Communiste Libertaire [OCL, Libertarian Communist Organization].)

[In *À la recherche d'un communisme libertaire*, 1984]

Notes

1. In 1969, Guérin had helped launch the Mouvement Communiste Libertaire (Libertarian Communist Movement), and two years later the MCL merged

with a number of other groups to create the Organisation Communiste Libertaire (Libertarian Communist Organization). This was the OCL's manifesto. [DB]

2.   Georges Fontenis (1920–2010) was one of the leading figures in the postwar revolutionary movement in France. He played an important role in the reconstruction and reform of the French anarchist movement (notably through the creation of the FCL), and in supporting those fighting for Algerian independence in the 1950s and 1960s. A prominent activist in May '68, he would go on to help (re)create a libertarian communist movement in the 1970s. He was also in later life one of the pillars of the Free Thought (La Libre Pensée) movement. Having joined the Union of Libertarian Communist Workers (UTCL) in 1980, he would subsequently become a member of Alternative Libertaire, and would remain a member until his death at the age of ninety. [DB]

■ APPENDIX II

The 1989 "Call for a Libertarian Alternative"

Since the winter of 1986–1987, struggles have followed one after the other. They demand to be given a combative and innovative expression.

The signatories of this appeal address all those women and men who think that under current social and political circumstances a new revolutionary alternative must be established. In our eyes, the creation of a revolutionary movement capable of building on and taking forward the newly revived struggles requires us to take two complementary paths:

- The formation of a new organization for a libertarian communism, which is what this appeal is proposing;
- The emergence of a vast and necessarily pluralist, anti-capitalist, self-management movement, to which organized libertarians will immediately contribute and where they will be active alongside other political tendencies.

We have entered a period of agitation and struggle that lays bare the inability of the Left and the union leaderships to respond to the aspirations of the population.

The "Socialist" Party (PS) manages capitalism, espouses its logic, and abandons any wish to transform society, even social democratic reformism. It opposes the interests of all popular strata. Under cover of "entering modernity" it wants to implement a political and social consensus with the Right and between the different classes. An electoral machine above all, the PS is a party of notables and technocrats where everything is decided at the summit, without any real democracy.

The French "Communist" Party (PCF) has not had a revolutionary perspective for some time. Its leadership makes use of social discontent, but the only model for society it has to offer is a still terribly bureaucratic USSR. It has a completely undemocratic organizational framework and imposes an unbearable grip on huge swaths of the union and social movements.

The union movement is confronted with the reemergence of struggles, but also with aspirations for self-organization that are being vigorously expressed. The chasm has never been so wide between unionized and non-unionized workers, between on the one hand union organizations that choose and self-manage their own battles, and on the other hand the fossilized union apparatuses which are often tied to the PS or the PCF.

The revolutionary, alternative, and ecological Left, with all its variants, does not propose a credible and attractive alternative. The top-down and centralized errors and myths inherited from Leninism continue to weigh heavily on some. On others, it is the strong temptation to integrate into institutional electoral politics and to constitute a "radical reformist axis" due to the repeated abandonment by social democracy of its project once it reaches power.

The balance sheet of the libertarian movement, such as it exists today, is no more positive and a debate over this point is necessary. For various reasons, we have not succeeded in putting forward a contemporary alternative. And many errors continue, here and there, to tarnish our image: divisions, disorganization, a certain sectarianism, sometimes an unreasoning cult of spontaneity, as well as the retreat into initiatives that have the merit of testifying to an ethical refusal of an alienating society, but which are nevertheless far too ideological and fail to provide the means of acting on social reality.

The signatories of this appeal affirm that there is room for a new libertarian struggle, one which is non-dogmatic, non-sectarian, and attentive to what is happening and what is changing in society. A struggle which is open and at the same time organized to be effective. A coherent, well-defined message, but one that is nevertheless not carved in stone, that is forever the object of reflection and renewal.

It is the aspirations expressed in the struggles for equality, self-organization, and the rejection of the neoliberal logic that lead us to this conclusion. It is also the road left open by the collapse of yesterday's dominant models: social democracy, Leninism, and Stalinism. Many militants would be open to the ideas of a resolutely anti-capitalist and libertarian current if it were able to engage with contemporary problems.

Finally, many anarchists and other anti-authoritarians have distinguished themselves, some very actively, in the recent battles in the union movement, in the student movement, in the fight against racism and for equality, and in support of the struggles of the Kanak people.[1] Many among them feel the movement is in need of modernization in order to pursue and strengthen their struggles, going beyond the structures and divisions within libertarianism that have most often been inherited from the past.

We propose to base ourselves on these practices in order to organize together a libertarian alternative that responds to the challenges of our time.

This perspective rests on a statement of fact: none of the current libertarian groups is capable of sufficiently representing this alternative. This objective statement in no way questions the value of the work of the various existing organizations. We do not reject them. On the contrary, we invite all organizations, local groups, reviews, and individuals to follow the process, to express themselves and participate in it. Their various experiences must not be rejected and forgotten. A new organization will be all the more rich if it were to succeed in bringing together and capitalizing on the many contributions that preceded it. But we have to do things differently if we are to respond to a new situation. The best way forward seems to us to be one that would take social and militant practice as its starting point as an element of a process under the control of rank-and-file individuals and collectives speaking from their experience, beyond the traditional divisions.

The initiative we are putting forward is therefore the work of a collective of individual signatories and we invite everyone to join in this process.

A contemporary affirmation of a libertarian communism is possible, elaborated on the basis of our social practice and an analysis of society that takes into account its profound economic, sociological, and cultural transformations:

- An aggressive, resolutely anti-capitalist, class struggle orientation in the conditions of today's society.
- A strategy of counter-powers where workers, the young, and the unemployed organize themselves and impose profound transformations through their autonomous struggles. This is a strategy that we oppose to that of change through institutional methods, the actions of parties and office-holders, and the illusion of political reformism. Basing ourselves on these struggles we can today defend a resolutely extra- and anti-parliamentary struggle without imprisoning ourselves in purely ideological campaigns.
- A self-management perspective and a combative strategy with revolution as its goal is practicable now: this libertarian struggle will base itself in social movements and the practice of its militants, practices that are broad-based, inclusive, and carried out without sectarianism. Practices that imply not only the self-management of struggles but also involvement in trade union activity in all of today's organizations (i.e., as much in the CFDT, the CGT, the FEN, and even FO as in the CNT and the independent unions).[2] But also a class-based approach outside as well as inside the workplace, in all aspects of life and society. Struggles against the patriarchal order. Against racism and for equality. Against imperialism, dictatorships, and apartheid. Against militarism. Against nuclear energy and for the defense of the environment. Struggles both of young people in education and those who are either unemployed or in casualized employment.

This libertarian affirmation anchored in present-day realities is very much within the lineage of one of the major currents in the history of the workers' movement.

We are referring—without dogmatism, without wishing to produce a naive apologia, and thus not without a critical spirit, but with a total independence of mind—to the anti-authoritarians of the First International, to the revolutionary syndicalists, to the anarcho-syndicalists, to the libertarian communists or anarchist-communists, without neglecting the contribution of council communism, trade unionism, self-management currents, feminism, and ecology. Without losing sight of the fact that it is the struggles of the workers themselves, the social movements of yesterday and today that sustain our reflections.

Bringing all of this heritage to bear on contemporary issues implies syntheses and much modernization on the way to a new political current facing towards the future.

We do not fetishize organization, but in order to elaborate and defend this struggle, organization is a necessity.

An organization means: the pooling of resources, experiences, different focuses, and political education; a place for debate for the elaboration of collective analyses; a means of quickly circulating information and of coordination; the search for a strategy which engages with present-day realities; a platform that expresses our identity.

We must seek a form of self-management of organization that is both democratic and federalist; that does not lead to confusion; that organizes convergences without denying differences; that offers a collective framework without hindering the free speech and activity of all. A self-managed organization, where the main orientations are decided democratically by all, by consensus or, if not, by vote. An effective organization with the necessary structures and means. An organization aimed at international practices and an international dimension at a time when Europe is in preparation.[3] It has always been the case that the anti-capitalist struggle cannot be contained within the narrow framework of each state.

We must also stress that we are not proposing a sect that will have no other end than its own growth. We must create a form of activism where commitment will not be all-consuming and alienating.

One of the assets of a new organization could be the publishing of a new type of press capable of reaching a broader public, which would be the expression of a current and an organization, certainly, but also an open tribune: a press self-managed by the militants; a wide network of external contributors; a press that would organize a portion of its columns as a permanent forum, open and pluralistic, where the militants of social movements and of revolutionary, libertarian, and self-management currents could express themselves.

(This Appeal was signed in May 1989 by around a hundred libertarians, political, trade union and social movement activists, members of various organizations and of none.)

[In *Pour le communisme libertaire*, 2003]

Notes

1. The Kanak are the indigenous people of New Caledonia (a French colonial possession in the Pacific). [DB]
2. As the editors of *Pour le communisme libertaire* (the 2003 Spartacus edition of the collection of articles on which the present volume is based) point out, the reference to the various trade union federations and confederations should be updated: "As much in the CGT and the FSU, even in FO, and perhaps the CFDT, as in the CNT and the SUD unions." The CNT (Confédération Nationale du Travail, or National Labour Confederation) was founded in 1946 and modelled on the Spanish CNT. The manifesto's general point is clear: the important thing is to fight for revolutionary practices in *all* the union organizations. [DB]
3. This text was written a few years after the Single European Act of 1986, which paved the way for the creation of a single market and single currency, but before their actual creation and the emergence of the European Union. [DB]

■ BIBLIOGRAPHY

English translations of works by Daniel Guérin
(in chronological order of first publication)

Fascism and Big Business (New York: Pioneer Press, 1939; Monad Press & Pathfinder Press for Anchor Foundation, 1973; Pathfinder Press, 1994); 1939 edition translated by Frances and Mason Merrill, introduced by Dwight Macdonald.

Negroes on the March: A Frenchman's Report on the American Negro Struggle (New York: George L. Weissman, 1956); translated and edited by Duncan Ferguson.

The West Indies and Their Future (London: Dennis Dobson, 1961); translated by Austryn Whainhouse.

'The Czechoslovak Working Class in the Resistance Movement' in Ken Coates (ed.), *London Bulletin* no. 9 (April 1969), pp. 15–18.

'The Czechoslovak Working Class in the Resistance Movement' in Ken Coates (ed.), *Czechoslovakia and Socialism* (Nottingham: Bertrand Russell Peace Foundation, 1969), pp. 79–89.

Anarchism: From Theory to Practice (New York: Monthly Review Press, 1970); translated by Mary Klopper, introduced by Noam Chomsky.

Class Struggle in the First French Republic: Bourgeois and Bras Nus, 1793–1795 (London: Pluto, 1977); translated by Ian Paterson.

The Writings of a Savage: Paul Gauguin, ed. Daniel Guérin (New York: Viking Press, 1978); translated by Eleanor Levieyx, introduced by Wayne Andersen.

100 Years of Labor in the USA (London: Ink Links, 1979); translated by Alan Adler.

Anarchism and Marxism (Sanday, Orkney: Cienfuegos Press, 1981); from a talk given in New York on 6 November 1973, with an introduction by Guérin.

'Lutte Ouvrière/Daniel Guérin: Trotsky and the Second World War' in *Revolutionary History* vol. 1, no. 3 (1988), available online at http://www.revolutionaryhistory.co.uk/rho103/dglt.html.

'Marxism and Anarchism' in David Goodway (ed.), *For Anarchism. History, Theory and Practice* (London: Routledge [History Workshop Series], 1989), pp. 109–26; translated by David Goodway.

The Brown Plague: Travels in Late Weimar and Early Nazi Germany (Durham, NC: Duke University Press, 1994); translated and introduced by Robert Schwartzwald.

'A Libertarian Marx?' in *Discussion Bulletin* [Industrial Union Caucus in Education, USA] no. 86 (November–December 1997), pp. 3–5.

No Gods No Masters: An Anthology of Anarchism (Edinburgh: AK Press, 1998, 2nd edition 2005), 2 vols., translated by Paul Sharkey.

■ ABOUT THE AUTHOR

Daniel Guérin (1904–1988) was a prominent member of the French left for half a century, and arguably one of the most original and most interesting. One of the first on the left to attach central importance to the struggle against colonialism, he became one of the best-known figures in anticolonial campaigns throughout the 1950s and '60s. He was also one of the first in France to warn of the rising dangers of fascism, publishing *The Brown Plague* in 1933 and *Fascism and Big Business* in 1936. He met Leon Trotsky in 1933 and would work with the Trotskyist resistance during the war; a respected member of the Fourth International during the 1940s, he was a close, personal friend of Michel Raptis (alias Pablo) until his death. His controversial, libertarian Marxist interpretation of the French Revolution, *Class Struggle in the First Republic, 1793–1797* (1945, 2nd ed. 1968) was judged by his friend C.L.R. James to be "one of the great theoretical landmarks of our movement" and by Sartre to be "one of the only contributions by contemporary Marxists to have enriched historical studies." Increasingly critical of what he saw as the authoritarianism inherent in Leninism, he influenced a generation of activists with his "rehabilitation" of anarchism through his *Anarchism* and the anthology *No Gods No Masters*, before playing a role in the resurgence of interest in Rosa Luxemburg and becoming better known for his attempts to promote a "synthesis" of Marxism and anarchism. He was also regarded by 1968 as the grandfather of the gay liberation movement in France and in the 1970s as a leading light in antimilitarist campaigns. His writings have been repeatedly republished both in French and in translation.

■ ABOUT THE EDITOR

David Berry has a BA in French and German from Oxford University, an MA in French Studies from the University of Sussex, and a DPhil in history, also from Sussex. He is currently a senior lecturer in politics and history at Loughborough University, UK. His publications include *A History of the French Anarchist Movement, 1917–1945* (AK Press, 2009); *New Perspectives on Anarchism, Labour and Syndicalism: The Individual, the National and the Transnational* (Cambridge Scholars Publishing, 2010), coedited with Constance Bantman; *Libertarian Socialism: Politics in Black and Red* (PM Press, 2011), coedited with Alex Prichard, Ruth Kinna, and Saku Pinta; and several journal articles and book chapters on Daniel Guérin. He is currently preparing a biography of Guérin to be published by PM Press.

■ ABOUT THE TRANSLATOR

Mitchell Abidor is the principal French translator for the Marxists Internet Archive. PM Press's collections of his translations include *Anarchists Never Surrender: Essays, Polemics, and Correspondence on Anarchism, 1908–1938* by Victor Serge; *Voices of the Paris Commune*; and *Death to Bourgeois Society: The Propagandists of the Deed*. His other published translations include *The Great Anger: Ultra-Revolutionary Writing in France from the Atheist Priest to the Bonnot Gang*; *Communards: The Paris Commune of 1871 as Told by Those Who Fought for It*; and *A Socialist History of the French Revolution* by Jean Jaurès.

ABOUT PM PRESS

PM Press was founded at the end of 2007 by a small collection of folks with decades of publishing, media, and organizing experience. PM Press co-conspirators have published and distributed hundreds of books, pamphlets, CDs, and DVDs. Members of PM have founded enduring book fairs, spearheaded victorious tenant organizing campaigns, and worked closely with bookstores, academic conferences, and even rock bands to deliver political and challenging ideas to all walks of life. We're old enough to know what we're doing and young enough to know what's at stake.

We seek to create radical and stimulating fiction and non-fiction books, pamphlets, T-shirts, visual and audio materials to entertain, educate, and inspire you. We aim to distribute these through every available channel with every available technology—whether that means you are seeing anarchist classics at our bookfair stalls; reading our latest vegan cookbook at the café; downloading geeky fiction e-books; or digging new music and timely videos from our website.

PM Press is always on the lookout for talented and skilled volunteers, artists, activists, and writers to work with. If you have a great idea for a project or can contribute in some way, please get in touch.

PM Press
PO Box 23912
Oakland, CA 94623
www.pmpress.org

FRIENDS OF PM PRESS

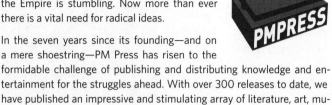

These are indisputably momentous times—the financial system is melting down globally and the Empire is stumbling. Now more than ever there is a vital need for radical ideas.

In the seven years since its founding—and on a mere shoestring—PM Press has risen to the formidable challenge of publishing and distributing knowledge and entertainment for the struggles ahead. With over 300 releases to date, we have published an impressive and stimulating array of literature, art, music, politics, and culture. Using every available medium, we've succeeded in connecting those hungry for ideas and information to those putting them into practice.

Friends of PM allows you to directly help impact, amplify, and revitalize the discourse and actions of radical writers, filmmakers, and artists. It provides us with a stable foundation from which we can build upon our early successes and provides a much-needed subsidy for the materials that can't necessarily pay their own way. You can help make that happen—and receive every new title automatically delivered to your door once a month—by joining as a Friend of PM Press. And, we'll throw in a free T-shirt when you sign up.

Here are your options:

- **$30 a month** Get all books and pamphlets plus 50 percent discount on all webstore purchases

- **$40 a month** Get all PM Press releases (including CDs and DVDs) plus 50 percent discount on all webstore purchases

- **$100 a month** Superstar—Everything plus PM merchandise, free downloads, and 50 percent discount on all webstore purchases

For those who can't afford $30 or more a month, we're introducing **Sustainer Rates** at $15, $10 and $5. Sustainers get a free PM Press T-shirt and a 50 percent discount on all purchases from our website.

Your Visa or Mastercard will be billed once a month, until you tell us to stop. Or until our efforts succeed in bringing the revolution around. Or the financial meltdown of Capital makes plastic redundant. Whichever comes first.

LIBERTARIAN SOCIALISM

Politics in Black and Red

Edited by Alex Prichard,
Ruth Kinna, Saku Pinta,
and David Berry

$26.95
ISBN: 978-1-62963-390-9
8.5x5.5 • 368 pages

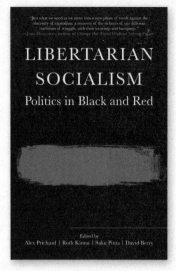

The history of anarchist-Marxist
relations is usually told as a history
of factionalism and division. These
essays, based on original research
and written especially for this
collection, reveal some of the en-
during sores in the revolutionary socialist movement in order to explore
the important, too often neglected left-libertarian currents that have
thrived in revolutionary socialist movements. By turns, the collection
interrogates the theoretical boundaries between Marxism and anarchism
and the process of their formation, the overlaps and creative tensions
that shaped left-libertarian theory and practice, and the stumbling blocks
to movement cooperation. Bringing together specialists working from
a range of political perspectives, the book charts a history of radical
twentieth-century socialism, and opens new vistas for research in the
twenty-first. Contributors examine the political and social thought of a
number of leading socialists—Marx, Morris, Sorel, Gramsci, Guérin, C.L.R.
James, Hardt and Negri—and key movements including the Situationist
International, Socialisme ou Barbarie and Council Communism. Analysis
of activism in the UK, Australasia, and the U.S. serves as the prism to
discuss syndicalism, carnival anarchism, and the anarchistic currents in
the U.S. civil rights movement.

Contributors include Paul Blackledge, Lewis H. Mates, Renzo Llorente,
Carl Levy, Christian Høgsbjerg, Andrew Cornell, Benoît Challand, Jean-
Christophe Angaut, Toby Boraman, and David Bates.